Praise for

The Essence of Humility

I love it. It speaks to my soul. I love what Lynn's done with the different aromas, the fruits, spices, and oils and how she's tied them into humility and love. Good job!
~Patricia Bradley,
Winner of **Inspirational Readers Choice Award**

Thank you for allowing me to be an early reader. I know this book on humility is going to bless many. (In Chapter 5) I was back on that bus with you. Love how you tied in the Word. Just perfect.
~April Rodgers,
Owner, **Reflecting Light Ministries**
https://aprilrodgers.com

When I read the text, I find myself slowing down. Breathing to enjoy the complexities woven into the simplicity. The author's passion as an advocate for children - for humanity - leans us closer to the Father's heart.
~Amanda Priefer
Advocate Manager (East Central), **Compassion® International**

Inspirational Collection for Women, Volume 3

The Essence of Humility

Live and Love Like Jesus

Lynn U. Watson

Cover Illustration by Allisha Mokry

Unless otherwise noted, all Scripture quotations are taken from the Holman Christian Standard Bible®, Copyright ® 1999, 2000, 2002, 2003, 2009 by Holman Bible Publishers. Used by permission. Holman Christian Standard Bible®, Holman CSB®, and HCSB® are federally registered trademarks of Holman Bible Publishers.

Other Bible Versions quoted:

Scripture quotations marked (NIV) are taken from **THE HOLY BIBLE, NEW INTERNATIONAL VERSION®, NIV®. Copyright © 1973, 1978, 1984, 2011 by Biblica, Inc.™ Used by permission. All rights reserved worldwide.**

Scripture quotations marked (NLT) are taken from the Holy Bible, New Living Translation, copyright © 1996, 2004, 2007 by Tyndale House Foundation. Used by permission of Tyndale House Publishers, Inc., Carol Stream, Illinois 60188. All rights reserved.

Scripture quotations marked (The Message) taken from **The Message.** Copyright © 1993, 1994, 1995, 1996, 2000, 2001, 2002. Used by permission of NavPress Publishing Group.

Scripture quotations marked (RSV) are from Revised Standard Version of the Bible, copyright © 1946, 1952, and 1971 National Council of the Churches of Christ in the United States of America. Used by permission. All rights reserved worldwide.

Scripture quotations marked (TLB) are from The Living Bible copyright © 1971 by Tyndale House Foundation. Used by permission of Tyndale House Publishers Inc., Carol Stream, Illinois 60188. All rights reserved. The Living Bible, TLB, and the The Living Bible logo are registered trademarks of Tyndale House Publishers.

Scripture quotations marked (TLV) are from Tree of Life (TLV) Translation of the Bible. Copyright © 2015 by The Messianic Jewish Family Bible Society.

Scriptures marked (VOICE) are taken from The Voice™. Copyright © 2008 by Ecclesia Bible Society. Used by permission. All rights reserved.

Scripture quotations taken from the Amplified® Bible (AMP). Copyright © 2015 by The Lockman Foundation Used by permission. www.Lockman.org

©Copyright 2018, Lynn U. Watson
Bartlett, Tennessee
All rights reserved.
ISBN: 978-1-7329281-0-7

*Mankind, He has told you what is good
and what it is the LORD requires of you:
to act justly,
to love faithfulness,
and to walk humbly with your God.
~Micah 6:8*

Contents

Introduction
A Letter to the Reader   13
A Few Hints for Using this Inspirational Volume   15
Newspaper Article about The Coffee Cottage   17
Cinnamah-Brosia's Profile & List of Friends
   (in order you meet them)   19
Chapter 1: Lavender/Humble Servants   27
Chapter 2: Olive Oil/Out of Your Comfort Zone   41
Chapter 3: Flax/Humble Obedience   57
Chapter 4: Almond/Watchfulness and Promise   73
Chapter 5: Chamomile/Trust The Word   93
Chapter 6: Eucalyptus/Restoration & Promises Delivered   113
Chapter 7: Coriander/Trusting God's Sufficiency   127
Chapter 8: Orange Blossom/Keep Your Words Humble   143
Chapter 9: Grapevine/Pruning for Abundance   159

A Few Parting Thoughts   173
Acknowledgements   177
Resources   179
Disclaimers   181
About the Author   183
Letter from Cinnamah-Brosia   184

Introduction

Thank you for taking the time to read the introduction. You'll be really glad you did, because it contains important information for my inspirational collection to make sense.

--Cinnamah-Brosia

Dear Friends,

My first lesson in humility for Volume 3 of Cinnamah-Brosia's Inspirational Collection came from an assumption. Right. Those are never a grand idea.

When God spoke to me about writing this book, he clearly gave me the subject: Love. I immediately headed to 1 Corinthians 13 – The Love Chapter of the Bible. Of course the book's title would be *The Essence of Love*. The end material of *The Essence of Joy* announced the new "Love" title coming in 2018.

And God laughed. I read 1 Corinthians 13 over and over again. It whispered "humility" over and over again. I called my dear friend – the one I consult with on every one of these books – and said, "You know what? Listen to this. Love is patient – humility. Love is kind – humility. Love is not arrogant – humility. You get the idea. Every single line of this beautiful passage comes down to the barest bones: humility." We both laughed a little, too. And we thanked God He clarified His instructions.

To live and love like Jesus requires us to humbly trust God and to humbly serve others.

In Philippians 2, the Apostle Paul presents a lengthy discourse on the humility of Christ. It begins like this:

> *If then there is any encouragement in Christ, if any consolation of love, if any fellowship with the Spirit, if any affection and mercy, fulfill my joy by thinking the same way, having the same love, sharing the same feelings, focusing on one goal. Do nothing out of rivalry or conceit, but in humility consider others as more important than yourselves. Everyone should look out not only for his own interests, but also for the interests of others.*
> ~Philippians 2:1-4

God led me to focus on humility along with more common everyday botanicals and plants – those familiar to us today. The fun came as I dug those plants from Scripture. I pray you enjoy the connections as much as I did uncovering them and connecting them to Jesus' life, and to a whole list of characters who lived on the pages of the Bible along with our contemporaries here in the 21st century.

Thank you for choosing *The Essence of Humility*. So very many titles out there shout to be read. I am humbled for you to spend time with me here. I have prayed for every one of you.

With the love of Jesus,

Lynn

NOTE: Cinnamah-Brosia (C-B) and friends share life lessons and experiences, emphasizing symbolism and attributes of each essential oil, spice, fruit, or plant featured in this volume, followed by an up close look at them in Scripture. We visit women of the Bible who experience the essence of these spices and fruits through lessons they learned, too. Icing on the cake comes in the form of Essence Droplets – "Fun Facts" and "Your Turn" – providing hands-on opportunities for you to make them more relevant in your life. The following pages offer you a few hints to navigate the books in C-B's Coffee Cottage collection.

A Few Hints for Using this Inspirational Volume

1. Cinnamah-Brosia and Friends Share Their Stories: These fictional characters introduce us to favorite fruits and aromas of the Christmas season, sharing their own stories about the essence in their lives. *(All the stories in the "Cinnamah-Brosia and Friends Share Their Stories" sections are based on events shared by real flesh and blood women. The stories have been fictionalized to fit our characters and timelines appropriately as well as to protect actual identities.)* They prepare us to discover the essence in Scripture and to meet a woman of the Bible whose own life exemplifies its attributes. "C-B" loves essential oils, baking, music, and God's Word. She spreads that love around. In these sections you will become better acquainted with her, learn what she's diffusing, and discover the café's special of the day, a song that's playing, and the Scripture verse she's posted. *(The oils chosen for diffusing may not be the same one featured for that fruit or spice, but they are ones typically readily available and complement the essence for that selection. Songs playing are an eclectic variety of old and new – mostly Christmas – songs. We hope you know and love many, and others will become new favorites. Just like "what's diffusing," each song was chosen to complement the subject matter.)*

2. The Essence in Scripture: a devotion that speaks of the fruit, spice or oil in context of Scripture. All personal stories included in "The Essence in Scripture" sections are drawn from the author's own experiences.

3. A Woman of the Bible Experiences the Essence: a devotion featuring a woman of the Bible who experiences some aspect of that essence in her life. All personal stories included in "A Woman of the Bible Experiences the Essence of" sections are drawn from the author's own experiences.

4. Essence Droplets: a collection of "Fun Facts" about each fruit, oil or spice; and "Your Turn" provides practical ways for you to incorporate them into your world.

Residing between the lines of Bible stories are real people like you and me. Consideration was made regarding how their lives may have been impacted by their culture and how they may have interacted with each other. Certainly, details may have been different than depicted, but the ones shared are definitely plausible. There's something to learn from each one. You may see each person in a different light than the picture you have in mind. We see each other in different lights, too. Thank you, Heavenly Father, You see us through the Light of Jesus.

On the next two pages, a news article from its opening provides a more detailed picture of The Coffee Cottage.

Many of the characters in the Cinnamah-Brosia stories were introduced in the first two volumes of this collection, **The Essence of Courage** and **The Essence of Joy**. Following the news article, and for your convenience, we've included a profile of Cinnamah-Brosia plus a list of characters in the order you first meet them in **The Essence of Humility**.

The Pearlville Weekly										October 4, 2016

Reno Complete: Cinnamah-Brosia's Coffee Cottage & Gift Shop Open

Cinnamah-Brosia's Coffee Cottage and Gift Shop hosted a well-attended grand reopening on Saturday, October 1. The coffee cottage is the former Miss Dot's Café. Gram and "C-B's" daughter, Kaitlyn, planned the redo prior to Miss Dot's passing. The walls have been refreshed in frothy cappuccino. Regulars will remember Sophia's Corner, a favorite gathering spot at the café. With a coat of white paint, the stone fireplace is still the cottage's focal point and even more inviting. The comfort of the gingerbread leather sofa and two overstuffed turquoise chairs filled with berry-trimmed vanilla accent pillows beckon you in. Kaitlyn's creativity has turned the old round wooden coffee table into a work of art. The pomegranate border was inspired by Gram's ambrosia recipe.

The addition of a gift shop provides convenience to customers. Currently, you will find garden items, artwork, books, jewelry, and kitchen gadgets. Kaitlyn is managing the gift shop and promises to keep the inventory fresh and exciting.

Cinnamah-Brosia's name is really Cinnamon. Her Gram, Miss Dot, prayed the name as a blessing over the child when she was three years old. The suffix "ah" in Hebrew means "of God." Cinnamon representing goodness, Miss Dot reinvented the name and trusted she would witness a harvest of the goodness of God in her granddaughter's life.

Everyone who visited Miss Dot's Café remembers her ambrosia. Cinnamah-Brosia recalled, "I requested her 'brosia every day during my childhood summer visits. Ambrosia is full of fruit reminding my Gram of the fruit of the Spirit. The name is a mouthful, I know, but she put the two words together. Others found ways to shorten it, but to Gram and Gramps I was always Cinnamah-Brosia. I really do love all that it meant to them."

With the transformation comes many opportunities for the people in the community to meet and hang out. The menu of scrumptious baked goods and both hot and chilled beverages guarantees a line forming every morning. The pleasant vintage space will be available for community events in the evenings. Cinnamah-Brosia's Coffee Cottage will serve guests from 6:30 AM to 2 PM each day.

It's easy to imagine Miss Dot proudly smiling down on her granddaughter today.

###

NOTE: *The selection above is a newspaper article (fictional, of course) that first appeared as introductory material in **The Essence of Courage**. It will help new readers understand more about Cinnamah-Brosia's Coffee Cottage, where she and her friends hang out.*

Cinnamah-Brosia's Profile

Birth Name: Cinnamon Amber Porter
Current Name: Cinnamon Amber (Porter) Fields
Nickname: Cinnamah-Brosia
Aliases: C-B, Cinnabro, Ms Cimmaba, Cinna-B, and many others her friends create
Birthday: May 14, 1970
Place of Birth: Pearlville, Missouri
Gender: Female
Eye Color: Green
Hair Color: Dark brown with rich red highlights
Height: 5'5"

Mother: Sandra Marie (Madison) Porter   1953
Father: Andrew (Andy) Robert Porter   1951
Siblings: Blossom Heather (Porter) Griffin 1971
   Stone Andrew Porter   1975
Maternal Grandmother: Dorothy Elizabeth (Perkins) Madison – a.k.a. Miss Dot) 1929-2016
Maternal Grandfather: Benjamin Henry Madison (Ben) 1926-2001
Education: Registered Nurse; completed nursing school May 1990
Husband: Jeremy Thomas Fields June 12, 1967
Wedding Date: May 12, 1990
Children: Kaitlyn Dorothy Fields, born November 10, 1994
      Aaron Thomas Fields, born May 22, 1995
      Caryn Joy Fields, born November 24, 1999
Transportation: bright red cruiser bicycle
Hobbies: aromatherapy, gardening, biking, all kinds of crafts (she rarely finds time for), reading, baking, entertaining, making others smile; she's dreaming of others she hasn't shared yet.

Miss Dot's Café opened in 1966. After her passing in early 2016, Miss Dot's will provided funding specifically to renovate the cottage. Her grandmother and Kaitlyn envisioned the changes, and

Cinnamah-Brosia promised Gram they would happen. The café would maintain its neighborly role in the community. A women's small group, formed several years earlier, continued to meet at the cottage during the construction phase. Although sometimes a challenge, they loved every minute of being part of, what they considered, community history in the making. In October 2016, Miss Dot's Café officially reopened as Cinnamah-Brosia's Coffee Cottage and Gift Shop.

Sophia's Corner: A stone fireplace as the backdrop, the corner is furnished with a gingerbread leather sofa and other comfy seating. The women's group meets here. It's rearranged a bit to be the "stage" area for musicians on Saturday nights when it opens as Fish and Beans Coffee House at the cottage. Sophia means wisdom in Greek, but the corner became known by that name in honor of the calico cat hanging around Miss Dot's Café. Gram called her Sophia, because she was wise enough to know where she would be loved and fed.

Fish and Beans Coffee House: In the early 1970's Gram and Gramps opened Miss Dot's Café on Saturday evenings as a coffee house hangout for teens. Local musicians led those who attended in Jesus movement songs popular at the time. Coffee, of course, is made from beans, and fish made the name because of its symbolic connection to Christianity. Cinnamah-Brosia and friends revived the tradition at the Coffee Cottage.

Sign displayed above The Coffee Cottage's menu board:
*Let all those you encounter leave happier
and better than they were before:
Have gentleness in your eyes – loving kindness in your smile.*
~Unknown

Cinnamah-Brosia's Friends –
in the order you meet them – See note at end of list.

*Pam – Pastor Gary's wife – In *The Essence of Joy*, she, Jane, Kaitlyn, and Cinnamah-Brosia are at The Coffee Cottage discussing some challenges following a teen star's recent concert. In *The Essence of Humility* she tells about an act of kindness toward her and Pastor Gary on a recent plane flight.

*Pastor Gary – In *The Essence of Courage* we meet him as the pastor of a local church. He had officiated at Cinnamah-Brosia and Jeremy's wedding. In *The Essence of Joy*, he and the Associate Pastor -- Pastor Able enjoy studying the Old and New Testaments together unlocking so many wonderful connections between the two. In *The Essence of Humility* he has an embarrassing situation on a trip. A stranger comes to his aid.

*Star – married to Tom – In *The Essence of Courage* Star faced the deaths of her mom and her twin brother within three weeks of each other. The love and kindness she experienced from Cinnamah-Brosia began to restore her faith. In *The Essence of Joy* we learn she and her husband Tom have been and still are raising their granddaughter, Grace. After the death of Star's mom, their wayward daughter asked for her grandmother's Bible, and a new chapter began. In *The Essence of Humility* she reminisces about C-B's kindness.

*Crystal – In *The Essence of Courage* we learned she had been coming to the café since she was a little girl (with her mom). She's married to Jeff and they have a little girl, Josie. In *The Essence of Joy* she's in attendance at the women's group holiday party. When we meet up with her in *The Essence of Humility* Crystal lets the group in on a little mission of hers to bring joy to others.

(Continued on page 22-25)

Haley – married to Dan – In *The Essence of Courage* the couple experienced a whole string of setbacks that had them questioning God. In *The Essence of Joy* she had an amazing encounter with Jesus. We first meet her in *The Essence of Humility* when the Tuesday night group is discussing random acts of kindness.

Carol – In *The Essence of Courage* she had a memory of Miss Dot's kindness to her when she lost a baby. She also brought Miss Alice (her mom and old friend of Miss Dot's who had moved away) to The Coffee Cottage to visit. In *The Essence of Joy* she offered Haley an excellent suggestion about a gift for Cinnamah-Brosia. When we first meet her in *The Essence of Humility* she talks about the fun she and her Aunt Norma had hiding gifts for strangers to find.

Jane – In *The Essence of Courage* we met Jane as the long-time friend of Miss Dot and Cinnamah-Brosia (and all the others). She helped in the café when it was Miss Dot's. She helps in The Coffee Cottage, too, and she leads the women's group meeting there. In *The Essence of Joy* we met her again serving a customer at The Coffee Cottage. From the beginning Cinnamah-Brosia lets us in on a secret: Jane is her most-amazing, cannot-live-without-her friend and co-worker. In *The Essence of Humility* she prepared a lesson about living and loving "outside our comfort zone." She has a story of her own that fits right in.

Miss Alice – Carol's mom – one of Gram's best friends. In *The Essence of Courage* she and husband, George, have retired and moved away from Pearlville. In *The Essence of Humility* we first encounter her when Jane tells her "outside-her-comfort-zone" story.

Kaitlyn – Cinnamah-Brosia and Jeremy's oldest daughter – In *The Essence of Courge* she planned the renovation of Miss Dot's Café into Cinnamah-Brosia's Coffee Cottage. In *The Essence of Joy* she is recently engaged to Trevor. She and her friends plans to shop for bridesmaids' dresses got interrupted when Trevor was involved in an automobile accident. Some Middle School girls have asked her to begin a small group for them. In *The Essence of Humility* she and the Middle School girls have a good-bye party for one of the friends, who is moving away, and a challenge arises among them.

Taylor – Friend in the Middle School girls' small group. She and her family are moving away.

*Carson – Laney's best friend. In *The Essence of Joy* she got involved in some trouble with drugs at a concert. She owed Laney a huge apology, and she delivered. Friend in the Middle School girls' small group. In *The Essence of Humility* she suggests to the whole group that they tell a lie to get an advantage.

Ella – Another friend in the Middle School girls' small group.

*Laney – Pam & Pastor Gary's twelve-year-old daughter – In *The Essence of Joy* she didn't get to go to a concert with her friends. In *The Essence of Humility* she is tempted by her friends again.

Julia – Another friend in the Middle School girls' small group.

*Susan – In *The Essence of Courage* she and husband Mark received a most unexpected answer to a long-time prayer request. In *The Essence of Humility* Susan and the others in the Tuesday evening group write notes to a child the group is sponsoring in Nicaragua.

*Gram – also known as Miss Dot. She is Cinnamah-Brosia's grandmother. She passed away three years ago, but reminders of this Godly lady will be found throughout *The Essence of Humility*, just as they were in *The Essence of Courage* and *The Essence of Joy*.

Maggie – She moved from Mexico to Pearlville recently, and is Carol's new neighbor. She and Carol make an instant connection. Carol introduces her to friends at the Coffee Cottage.

Lynn – She writes the books, but this is her first personal visit to the Coffee Cottage. Cinnamah-Brosia and Jane laugh at the thought, because they know she made them up.

Deborah – Silently in the background of the first two books, this very quiet friend opens up to the group with a special testimony of how God worked in the lives of her and her son, Steven, following her divorce.

Lily – A seven-year-old in **The Essence of Courage**. Her family decided to be the church liaison for a missionary family. Lily had lots of questions about their little girl of the same age. In **The Essence of Joy** she had many questions about adoption. She's a big nine-year-old (almost ten-year-old) now. In **The Essence of Humility** she and her best friend, Molly, learn a lesson about using their words carefully, when their moms hear them discussing an incident at school.

Molly – Lily's best friend. In **The Essence of Joy** Lily's family had just adopted a little girl. In **The Essence of Humility** she and Lily learn a lesson from an incident at school.

Mandy – Lily's mom – In **The Essence of Courage** she and Lily are in The Coffee Cottage. They told Cinnamah-Brosia about their new connection with a missionary family. In **The Essence of Joy** she was present during a cookie-baking day with Lily and her friends. In **The Essence of Humility** she and her friend Amber and their daughters, Lily and Molly visit the Coffee Cottage after school.

Amber – Molly and Oliva's mom. In **The Essence of Joy** she and her husband adopted baby Olivia. She answered questions about adoption for Molly's curious young frineds. In **The Essence of Humility** she and her friend Mandy and their daughters, Lily and Molly visit the Coffee Cottage after school.

Vickie – One of the friends in the Tuesday night group back when the Coffee Cottage was still Miss Dot's Café. She and her husband moved several states away before the Coffee Cottage opened. In *The Essence of Humility* she makes a surprise visit, and she has a huge "lesson-learned" story to share.

NOTE: Many of these friends were first introduced in *The Essence of Courage* and *The Essence of Joy*. They are marked with an asterisk (*). Those introduced for the first time in The Essence of Humility are not.

You are personally invited to join Cinnamah-Brosia and her friends throughout the year by visiting our blog: https://LynnUWatson.com/blog. Lynn posts regular updates, and you'll find a menu board there too, with links to the recipes featured at Cinnamah-Brosia's Coffee Cottage.

Chapter 1

Humble Servants

Cinnamah-Brosia and Friends Share About
Lavender
Generous Portions of Kindness

Diffusing today: Lavender, peppermint, and lemon
Aromatic influence: Helps create a warm and stimulating environment filled with a sense of love, peace and well-being
Daily Delight: Lavender Lemon Loaf Cake
Musically: **How Beautiful** (Twila Paris)
Verse of the Day:
> *The generous will prosper;*
> *those who refresh others will themselves be refreshed.*
> ~Proverbs 11:25 (NLT)

Pam grabbed our attention at our Tuesday night group gathering.

"Girls, I just have to share this amazing story. On our trip to Dallas last week, Gary got so sick. Our small jet flew straight into a terrible lightning storm. Fear etched the faces of everyone aboard the plane. Most bowed their heads and prayed as the plane bounced through the turbulence. Gary heaved all over himself, the aisle, me, and anything else in the path – so embarrassing for both of us! The only flight attendant, a very young man, hardly knew what to do with so many frightened passengers, much less take care of Gary's needs.

"Fellow passengers amazed me — especially moms with babies — who quickly dug through their bags and diaper bags. They tossed us items to help with clean up and to help settle Gary's stomach. The flight attendant finally managed to bring a warm wet cloth, but we needed a cold one. Bless one dear lady who tossed me what looked like an ice pack. It was cabin-temperature. Not much help. Someone said, 'Bend it like one of those glow light sticks.' Sure enough, it quickly chilled – a Godsend, for sure.

"We never learned the identities of those who provided all that we needed. I did know she listened to the small still voice that prompted her to share what she had. I suspected it was an important item she carried for a specific reason, and she offered it to us."

Pam's story launched a discussion about random acts of love and kindness – ones we had received, given, or observed.

Star reminded us of the time I (Cinnamah-Brosia) caught her off guard with loving kindness. "I felt so undeserving of her special attention and gifts, but so grateful for them when Mom and my brother died." (The original story is found in ***The Essence of Courage***.)

Crystal spoke up. "I have never told anyone about this. Since I love to clip coupons, I leave some on the shelves where the product is located in the grocery store. I'm blessed to bring a kindness to someone who doesn't know me."

A few of the ladies were surprised to learn the coupons they found were from Crystal. Lots of thanks went around the circle.

Haley reminisced, "Dan and I received a rather sizable gift card when we were going through so many setbacks a couple years ago. It was sent anonymously. The only thing we knew was it had been mailed from the church. What a blessing!"

Jane asked, "Remember our friend Vickie who moved away a few years ago? I told all of you how she broke her ankle so badly several months ago. I heard from her this week. Still in healing mode, she mentioned it takes all the energy she and Jack have to get household tasks done and make it to her therapy appointments. Some anonymous "angels" came by last week and cleaned up leaves and debris from their yard. They wished they knew whom to thank."

Carol remembered, "I loved shopping with my Aunt Norma. She and I wrote little notes that said, 'God loves you! Here's a little happy for your day.' We wrapped them around $5 bills. While we shopped and when we knew no one was looking we tucked the notes under jewelry box lids. We laughed and thought of the smiles on the faces of those making the discoveries."

There I sat, humbled by the abundant outpourings of love, and especially when Star shared the story of the Princess party again.

"Ladies, you know I believe God's heart is full when we offer our lives, our time, our possessions, our talents, and our best creative endeavors to touch another's life. I'm amazed when they are done anonymously, but what a blessing to share how we touch each other's lives – even the lives of strangers with His love. And how they touch ours."

Have you been prompted to act on a seemingly silly prompt? Do you recognize the nudge coming from the Holy Spirit's leading? Are you encouraged to respond? It may be just the touch from Him that someone else needs?

God knows where we travel – the steps we take each day. He allows those steps to cross the paths of others needing His love. How do we meet them? Be encouraged to slow down and listen for His still small voice.

> *But the lovers of God walk on the highway of light, and their way shines brighter and brighter until they bring forth the perfect day.*
>
> ~Proverbs 4:18 (TPT)

The Essence of Lavender in the Bible
With a Towel and a Basin

Botanical Name: Lavendula
Native to: dry rocky areas of Mediterranean, Africa, Asia and India;
essential oil steam distilled from flowering tops

"When is the last time Jesus asked you to wash someone's feet?" asked the pastor, as he began his sermon on Jesus washing the disciples feet. He expected no one had been asked to do that in a very long time — or ever. I thought, "He requests that of me almost everyday!" My other job — when I'm not writing or gathering research for my writing — is reflexologist. Are you familiar with the term? To keep things simple we will say, "I rub feet for a living."

Most people arrive for their appointment with very clean feet. Embarrassed, they beg forgiveness if their feet lack a recent pedicure. Very rarely, but it does happen, someone comes with dirty feet or feet otherwise "a mess." Everyone receives equal attention and care. I pray the client experiences a touch of Jesus' love through my hands. A reflexology map of the feet pictures the whole body reflected in our feet. This quote appears on the homepage of my website.

> "When you touch a body, you touch the whole person, the intellect, the spirit, and the emotions."
> ~Jane Harrington[1]

I am awed and humbled over each person who entrusts me with the responsibility. Jesus instructed His disciples and us, too, to make serving others a regular practice.

---

[1] https://www.inspirationalstories.com/quotes/jane-harrington-when-you-touch-a-body-you-touch/ (Accessed 9/27/2018)

And since I, your Lord and Teacher, have washed your feet, you ought to wash each other's feet. I have given you an example to follow. Do as I have done to you.
~John 13:14-15

Jesus placed no importance on rank or position. He humbled Himself often. His foot-washing service offers the perfect example. From my vantage point at people's feet, I understand why. The humble position reinforces the fact not one of us is better than another. Jesus means for all of us to serve and love one another.

I tell you the truth, slaves are not greater than their master. Nor is the messenger more important than the one who sends the message. Now that you know these things, God will bless you for doing them.
~John 13:16-17

Hearing clients share benefits they received from reflexology ranks high on my blessing list. When they exclaim over my "magic fingers," I point out my learned-skill-set along with my willingness for God to use me in this way. He favored me with a giftedness or aptitude, but the benefits all come from Him. I lay no claim to be anything more than a conduit of God's love.

What does God regularly ask of you where you are required to acknowledge we are all equal before Him? Has He placed you in a position of humility as you served people others considered to be the "less-thans" of our world? When given opportunities to share my reflexology with them, the rewards are even sweeter.

The common foot-washing rituals we read about in the Bible call for more than water and a towel. Gather more insight from the next devotion about the sinful woman who washed Jesus' feet with her hair and what lavender had to do with it.

A Woman of the Bible Humbly Serves

Lavender, Nard, and a Whole Lot of Love

Forgiveness is the smell that lavender gives out when you tread on it.[2]
~Mark Twain

> *One of the Pharisees asked Jesus to have dinner with him, so Jesus went to his home and sat down to eat. When a certain immoral woman from that city heard he was eating there, she brought a beautiful alabaster jar filled with expensive perfume. Then she knelt behind him at his feet, weeping. Her tears fell on his feet, and she wiped them off with her hair. Then she kept kissing his feet and putting perfume on them.*
>
> ~Luke 7:36-38 (NLT)

Allow me to share some interesting facts about the ancient foot-washing custom.

> *Ceremonial foot washing usually involved marking the toe with blood or oil to symbolize either consecration or the cleansing of the entire person. This type of ritual was considered important before entering God's house.*
>
> *Persian custom even included kissing of those of superior rank and falling at the feet of those of lower rank. It too was considered an act of submission, respect, gratitude, supplication, neediness, and humility and was used on all sorts of occasions.*[3]

---

[2] https://quotefancy.com/quote/862087/Mark-Twain-Forgiveness-is-the-smell-that-lavender-gives-out-when-you-tread-on-it (Accessed 9/27/2018)

[3] http://biblefeet.blogspot.com/2010/03/curious-custom-of-ceremonial-foot.html (Accessed 2/6/2018)

At least two different women anointed Jesus' feet during His ministry. Mary of Bethany anointed Him in her home six days before Passover (John 12:1-3). Two days before Passover, a sinful woman anointed Jesus' feet at the home of a Pharisee (Mark 14:1-9). Tradition calls the second Mary a prostitute. Today we focus on the sinful woman.

The sinful woman kissed Jesus feet. She knelt behind Him at His feet and allowed her tears to run over the feet that would walk the long road to the cross for her.

> *Once a Pharisee named Simon invited Jesus to be a guest for a meal.*
>
> *Picture this:*
> *Just as Jesus enters the man's home and takes His place at the table, a woman from the city—notorious as a woman of ill repute—follows Him in. She has heard that Jesus will be at the Pharisee's home, so she comes in and approaches Him, carrying an alabaster flask of perfumed oil. Then she begins to cry, she kneels down so her tears fall on Jesus' feet, and she starts wiping His feet with her own hair. Then she actually kisses His feet, and she pours the perfumed oil on them.*
> ~Luke 7:36-38 (Voice)

While customary for the lowest servant to wash guests' feet, criticism ensued that Jesus allowed "such a woman" to even touch Him. In their opinion her status slipped below that of the lowest servant. And she lacked a proper invitation. The woman heard news Jesus would attend the party, and she sought Him out.

Her actions whispered fragrant wisps of humility usually attributed to spikenard. Lavender grew all over the Mediterranean region. Some who have studied its use in

Biblical context believe lavender (from the root word 'larve' — to wash) may have been mixed with nard to create the oil the woman used.[4]

Not one of the invited dinner guests or the host stooped low enough to offer to wash Jesus' feet – so beneath their status. Yikes! By not serving Jesus, they elevated themselves above God. While the other guests busied themselves with their own self-importance, Jesus harbored no worries about being equal with God.

Jesus, Who is God, later washed the disciples feet. I believe He would have showed His love for the woman by washing her feet, too.

Apostle Paul reminds us of Jesus' humble heart in Philippians. He encourages us to have this same mindset as Jesus.

If you find any comfort from being in the Anointed, if His love brings you some encouragement, if you experience true companionship with the Spirit, if His tenderness and mercy fill your heart; then, brothers and sisters, here is one thing that would complete my joy — come together as one in mind and spirit and purpose, sharing in the same love. Don't let selfishness and prideful agendas take over. Embrace true humility, and lift your heads to extend love to others. Get beyond yourselves and protecting your own interests; be sincere, and secure your neighbors' interests first. In other words, Remember: Though He was in the form of God, He chose not to cling to equality with God; But He poured Himself out to fill a vessel brand new; a servant in form and a man indeed. The very likeness of humanity, He humbled

---

[4] http://blog.jerseylavender.co.uk/?p=850 (Accessed 9/28/2018)

Himself, obedient to death— a merciless death on the cross! So God raised Him up to the highest place and gave Him the name above all. So when His name is called, every knee will bow, in heaven, on earth, and below. And every tongue will confess "Jesus, the Anointed One, is Lord," to the glory of God our Father!
~Philippians 2:1-11 (Voice)

Written later, the sinful woman never heard these words, but she witnessed Jesus' life. She chose to offer an act of the humble servant heart Jesus modeled. In her case, someone of far "lesser status" than the dinner guests came to do what they refused to stoop low enough to do. And it bothered them that this "pathetic" woman claimed the job. Jesus was well pleased with her actions.

How do you think that made the invited guests feel? Some of them, no doubt, pushed their noses higher and further out of joint. Did some guests quietly contemplate what had just happened, and learn a new lesson in humility?

What tasks have you seen as beneath you? What lessons has God taught you in those moments?

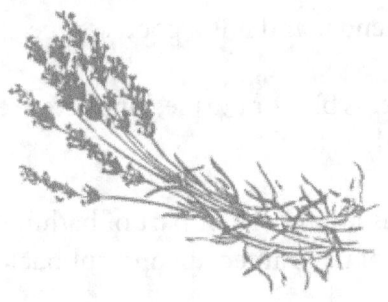

Lavender Essence Droplets

God makes fun of those who make fun of the truth but gives loving-favor to those who have no pride.
~~Proverbs 3:34 (NLT)

Fun Facts:

- Lavender buds are covered in tiny hairs.[5]

- Great to use in cooking meats and sweets. Most commonly dried flower buds are used for this. The leaves may be, also.[5]

- Lavender was used in the mummification process in Egypt.[5]

- During the Black Plague, which hit London in the 16th century, lavender oil and alcohol were taken as a way to ward off the disease. Bunches of lavender were sold in the streets in an attempt to ease the smell of the dead and dying.[6]

- Bees love lavender and it is a good source of honey.[6]

- Most lavender is blue or purple, but there are varieties available in pink and yellow, too.[7]

- Lavender was an important part of bathing rituals in Ancient Rome because of its disinfectant and antibacterial properties.[7]

---

[5] https://www.countryliving.com/gardening/g2525/lavender-facts/ (Accessed 9/27/2018)
[6] https://greenblender.com/smoothies/4773/lavender-facts (Accessed 9/27/2018)
[7] http://justfunfacts.com/interesting-facts-about-lavender/ (Accessed 9/27/2018)

- During Medieval times, people were divided on the properties of lavender regarding love. Some would claim that it could keep the wearer chaste, while others claimed just the opposite—touting its aphrodisiac qualities.[8]

- Lavender is in the mint family.[8]

- Lavender, like citronella, has a fragrance that repels insects.[6]

Short history lesson about lavender essential oil:

> "In 1910 French chemist and scholar René-Maurice Gattefossé discovered the virtues of the essential oil of lavender. Gattefossé badly burned his hand during an experiment in a perfumery plant and plunged his hand into the nearest tub of liquid, which just happened to be lavender essential oil. He was later amazed at how quickly his burn healed and with very little scarring. This started a fascination with essential oils and inspired him to experiment with them during the First World War on soldiers in the military hospitals."[9]

Your Turn:

- Drop dried crushed lavender buds on your carpet before vacuuming. They will add a fresh scent.[6]

- Use dried lavender and lavender essential oils to make calming and soothing bath salts. Need a recipe? Check this link.[10]

---

[8] Connie and Alan Higley, Reference Guide for Essential Oils, (Spanish Fork, Utah: Abundant Health, 1996-2012, Thirteenth Edition revised January 2012)
[9] http://roberttisserand.com/2011/04/gattefosses-burn/ (Accessed 9/27/2018)
[10] https://preparednessmama.com/lavender-harvest/ (Accessed 9/27/2018)

- The same website with the recipe for bath salts, also gives directions for creating a lovely lavender wand. These would be beautiful for a wedding or a shower or other springtime party.[10]

- If lavender by itself is relaxing, think about combining it with chamomile tea in this recipe for homemade soap.[11]

- Freshen your laundry with lavender linen spray and/or lavender sachets. DIY instructions are found at this link.[12]

[11] https://apumpkinandaprincess.com/lavender-chamomile-tea-soap/ (Accessed 9/27/2018)
[12] https://www.gardeningchannel.com/3-ways-to-use-lavender-flowers-to-freshen-laundry/ (Accessed 9/27/2018)

Chapter 2

Olive Oil
Out of Your Comfort Zone

Cinnamah-Brosia and Friends Share About

Olive Oil Love When It's Uncomfortable

Diffusing Today: Lemon and Fennel
Aromatic Influence: May be invigorating and offer a sense of courage
Daily Delight: Fennel Honey Cake
Musically: *Voice of Truth* (Casting Crowns)
Verse of the Day:

> But He said to me,
> "My grace is sufficient for you,
> for power is perfected in weakness."
> Therefore, I will most gladly boast all the more about my
> weaknesses, so that Christ's power may reside in me.
> ~2 Corinthians 12:9

"Listen, Cinnamah," Jane whispered. Casting Crowns sang *Voice of Truth* — coming from our playlist at the cottage while she and I prepared for our guests today.

As the song concluded Jane spoke. "Those words about stepping outside our comfort zone — I've heard them over and over this past week as I prepared a lesson on the subject for our group tonight. This song failed to cross my mind until this moment.

"Remember the story about Ezekiel eating the scrolls that tasted like honey? I read it this morning. God offered Ezekiel those scrolls to encourage him. God asked Ezekiel to operate way outside his comfort zone, but God was there. The hard-hearted children of Israel rebelled, but God told Ezekiel to go tell them what He expected of them, even if they didn't listen.

God filled Ezekiel in on the details of His assignment first. Imagine the fear Ezekiel experienced! Here's what God said to him. Let me grab my Bible so I can read it to you.

> He said to me: "Son of man, I am sending you to the Israelites, to the rebellious pagans who have rebelled against Me. The Israelites and their ancestors have transgressed against Me to this day. The children are obstinate and hardhearted. I am sending you to them, and you must say to them, 'This is what the Lord God says.' Whether they listen or refuse to listen — for they are a rebellious house — they will know that a prophet has been among them."
>
> ~Ezekiel 2:3-5

"God already placed the Holy Spirit in Ezekiel when He gave these instructions. Still, I envision Ezekiel's concern about Israelites spitting on him, laughing at him, spreading rumors about him, or even stoning him. I see his whole body shaking in his sandals after he received this word. God warned Ezekiel about potential for his own disobedience.

> "And you, son of man, listen to what I tell you: Do not be rebellious like that rebellious house."
>
> ~Ezekiel 2:8a

"God handed Ezekiel scrolls to eat. The tough words he would speak to the Israelites tasted like honey in his mouth as he ate the rolls of inscribed skins. God continued to encourage Ezekiel in preparation for his assignment:

> "I have made your forehead like a diamond, harder than flint. Don't be afraid of them or discouraged by the look on their faces, even though they are a rebellious house."
>
> ~Ezekiel 3:9

"Following this encounter Ezekiel experienced a powerful vision from God: living creatures with wings and wheels rumbled and moved about. Ezekiel continued to fear even to the point of being angry. His heart needed more grace and encouragement. Eventually, Ezekiel went as God asked of him."

I saw Jane's excitement over this revelation. "I admit, when I think about Ezekiel eating those scrolls tasting like honey, I don't always remember the rest of the story. He really did have to step outside his comfort zone, and he balked, too, like we do when God assigns us deeds we feel ill equipped to handle. Ezekiel operated in God's strength, not his own.

"How many other Bible characters faced big challenges outside their comfort zones? David killed a giant with a sling and a stone. Daniel refused to eat the king's rich food or bow down to him, and he landed in the lion's den. Paul spent much time imprisoned for preaching the Gospel. And the list goes on and on."

"Your right C-B. So, Sunday when Pastor Gary shared a request for volunteers to visit with prisoners at the women's facility, the Holy Spirit stirred in my heart. I said, 'No way, God. That's just way outside my comfort zone. Maybe I could make cookies.' This subject keeps coming up. God and I are in a wrestling match about this one."

"If Gram were still here, she would remind us again of Ephesians 2:10 about now. Here it is from *The Message*."

> He creates each of us by Christ Jesus to join him in the work he does, the good work he has gotten ready for us to do, work we had better be doing.
> ~Ephesians 2:10 (MSG)

"You are so right! She would! And did you just preview all of tonight's lesson for me?" I asked with a grin.

Jane went on. "The whole preparation for this lesson took me back many years when the Spirit nudged me out of my comfort zone. It seems like such a little thing now, but at the time I was in my early 20's, very young in my faith, and concerned about the reactions of others. Miss Alice was in her 50's back then. I knew who she was, but didn't know her well at all. Her mom passed away a few weeks earlier. Carol had nursery duty that morning. Miss Alice sat all alone.

I noticed tears in her eyes when the next hymn was announced: "*What a Friend We Have in Jesus.*"

"The Spirit whispered: 'Get up and sit by her.'

"I talked back. 'Are you kidding me, God? What will people think about this young girl bold enough to go comfort an older lady? What do I have to offer?' I ignored the prompt. It didn't help. It came again, this time with more urgency. I had to do it. I sat down next to Miss Alice and held her hand. Her tears flowed as the congregation sang, and slowly the peace of the Holy Spirit washed over both of us. She hugged me and thanked me. It had been her mom's favorite hymn.

"What shocked me most – five different people came to me later and thanked me for loving on Miss Alice."

The Essence of Olive Oil in the Bible

He Loved Far Outside His Comfort Zone

Botanical Name: Olea europaea
Native to: Mediterranean Basin,
Arabian Peninsula, Southern Asia, China,
Canary Islands, and Reunion
Olives are cold pressed to produce olive oil

Called upon to care for a family member for a week following invasive surgery launched me into a galaxy far, far away from my comfort zone. If one occupation existed to which I had absolutely no aspirations it was nursing. Agony reigned supreme in many moments. I remained grateful for His grace to walk that road with a joyful spirit. Serving outside our comfort zone presents opportunity for humility to flourish.

In His humanity, Jesus faced challenges outside His comfort zone, too.

> *Since we have a great High Priest, Jesus, the Son of God who has passed through the heavens from death into new life with God, let us hold tightly to our faith. For Jesus is not some high priest who has no sympathy for our weaknesses and flaws. He has already been tested in every way that we are tested; but He emerged victorious, without failing God. So let us step boldly to the throne of grace, where we can find mercy and grace to help when we need it most.*
> ~Hebrews 4:14-16 (Voice)

Scenes from Thursday of Passover week suggest Jesus struggled outside His comfort zone, too — at least His human comfort zone. He served His disciples. He washed their feet. He ate the Passover meal with them. As He shared the first Lord's Supper with them, He proclaimed His body and blood broken for them. He foretold His betrayal. Judas departed the fellowship of the group.

Following the meal Jesus and His disciples approached the Mount of Olives. Jesus prayed and invited His friends to pray with Him. Instead, they slept while He ventured further up the mountain to speak with His Father. In His prayer we hear Jesus say:

> *Jesus: Father, this is the last thing I want. If there is any way, please take this bitter cup from Me. Not My will, but Yours be done.*
>
> ~Matthew 26:39 (Voice)

Luke's words, deliver more evidence of how far outside His comfort zone Jesus really felt.

> *Then a messenger from heaven appeared to strengthen Him. And in His anguish, He prayed even more intensely, and His sweat was like drops of blood falling to the ground.*
>
> ~Luke 22:43-44 (Voice)

He asked for another way – anything. Yet, in spite of His discomfort, He yielded to the will of His Father. He loved His Father, and He loved every one of us – that much!

He and the Father loved us perfectly and without condition. They sacrificed to ensure our eternity with them. The ultimate sacrifice of Jesus sets the standard for the humility and trust God requires of us to accomplish the work He has for us.

> *I have been crucified with the Anointed One — I am no longer alive — but the Anointed is living in me; and whatever life I have left in this failing body I live by the faithfulness of God's Son, the One who loves me and gave His body on the cross for me.*
>
> ~Galatians 2:20 (Voice)

We easily think a task is not for us. It lies way outside our giftedness and our comfort zone. We say, "I know God meant it for someone else."

But God may be saying, "I know this pushes your limits, but my gift to you is the grace and empowerment to accomplish the task I've asked of you."

> *Whatever I have, wherever I am, I can make it through anything in the One who makes me who I am.*
> *~Philippians 4:13 (MSG)*

I love the family member who needed my help. Jesus loves her, too. Compelled by love, I agreed to take on the task asked of me. I learned more of Jesus' humility and His love for me. God empowered Jesus, the Man, to suffer a brutal death He preferred to avoid. His grace and love empowered me to accomplish a much simpler task, but one I preferred to avoid, as well.

When has God asked you to serve outside your comfort zone? How did you respond? How did God meet you there? Do you have a fresh and renewed appreciation for the humility and the love it required of Him to purchase our redemption with His own life?

A Few More Thoughts on Olives

> *The dove brought Noah an olive-leaf after the flood, to show that the waters had abated off earth, and that peace had been restored. Since then, olive leaves symbolize the hope for peace, the hope that peace takes the place of all the evil and destruction of the world, the hope that we live in a safe and quiet place.*[13]

Jesus' brutal death (and resurrection) are our guarantee of hope for eternity. The events leading to His most humble act of love occurred on the Mount of Olives.

Olive trees covered the Mount of Olives. Olives and the products coming from them have provided an important commodity in Israel for millennia.

> *"The olive oil had five main uses in Bible days: food, illumination, ointment, soap, and leather and metal preservative."* [14]

> *The mount has been the site of significant events of the Old and New Testaments. Jesus taught on the Mount of Olives — including his parable of the 10 virgins, five of them being unprepared because they ran out of oil. Bethany, the home of His friends — Mary, Martha, and Lazarus — was on the Eastern side of the Mount of Olives. Jesus prayed on the Mount of Olives. He was betrayed and arrested on the Mount of Olives.*

---

[13] https://www.jpost.com/PromoContent/The-Olive-in-the-Jewish-and-Israeli-culture-193416 (Accessed 9/27/2018)
[14] Lytton John Musselman, Figs, Dates, Laurel, and Myrrh: Plants of the Bible and the Quran, (Portland, Oregon: Timber Press, 2007. Page 210

He ascended to heaven from the Mount of Olives. He will return on the Last Day on the Mount of Olives, splitting the mountain in two from East to West.[15]

---

[15] https://www.gotquestions.org/Mount-of-Olives.html (Accessed 9/27/2018)

A Woman of the Bible Humbly Chooses Outside Comfort Zone

Tale of Two Moms

*If we're growing,
we're always going to be out of our comfort zone.*[16]
~John C. Maxwell

Moms, to what lengths will you go to protect your children? A quick internet search turned up many stories of moms who took heroic actions. One used her bare hands to pry open the mouth of a crocodile, freeing her daughter's leg from its grasp. Another threw a mattress over her three children, and laid on top of it to hold it down when a tornado destroyed their home. The children lived. The mother did not. Still another lifted a car as neighbors pulled her son from under the wheels, which had fallen on him. Love for our children drives us to do whatever it takes to keep them safe. Every one of these actions, though, would put me well outside of my comfort zone and require me to humbly rely on God to empower my love for my children. Links are provided below to read these stories and more like them.[16, 17]

An Old Testament story puts humility and love for our children in great perspective. In 1 Kings 3:16-28 two moms requested King Solomon's ruling when a dispute arose between them. Mom #1 crushed her son in her sleep. Another woman living in the same home, also had a baby.

---

[16] https://quotefancy.com/quote/192225/John-C-Maxwell-If-we-re-growing-we-re-always-going-to-be-out-of-our-comfort-zone (Accessed 9/27/2018)

[17] https://www.theloop.ca/12-moms-who-defied-death-to-save-their-children/ (Accessed 9/27/2018)

[18] https://www.womansday.com/life/real-women/a1522/moms-whove-risked-it-all-to-save-their-kids-106576/ (Accessed 9/27/2018)

Mom #1 exchanged the infants while Mom #2 slept. When Mom #2 awoke to feed her baby, she realized the dead child in her arms was not hers. A huge argument erupted. The women appealed to Solomon to settle their dispute.

Solomon heard them out and asked for a sword. He proposed a solution. If he sliced the living baby in two pieces, each mom received part of a child. Mom #2 begged Solomon to give the baby to Mom #1 rather than hurt the child. Mom #1 decided the child should be cut in two so he would belong to neither of them. You see where this is going. Solomon gave the baby to Mom #2. He determined the baby was hers because of her compassion and willing sacrifice to protect him.

Imagine the emotions? Mom #1 is in mourning. She is also angry. There's no humility in unresolved anger. Her actions demonstrated arrogance and revenge. She suffered significant loss, and her pain spiked beyond comprehension for most of us. If you have faced devastating loss in your life, you understand her emotions all too well. In moments of pain inflicted by another, thoughts of how we might hurt them back, easily creep in. That equals not-so-sweet revenge.

Mom #2 suffered a great wrong. If these two women continued living in the same house, will Mom #2 find forgiveness for her roommate? Her first response wrestled with justice. While they stood before Solomon awaiting his wisdom, Mom #2 saw devastating danger to her child. The child would die under Solomon's proposed solution. What humility and pain it took for Mom #2 to ask the child be given to the woman who had wronged her so mercilessly. Mom #1 continued her craziness. She insisted the child be cut up – both would be childless.

Mom #2 most certainly questioned her own sanity in even suggesting the arrangement. What anxiety she endured while Solomon decided. If any tears remained in her, did she cry every one of them out over the floor of his palace? Or was she left totally numb? From her humble act Solomon realized the truth. Mom #2's humility and love saved her child, and restored him to her.

Rest assured Mom #2 was out of her comfort zone, but outside of her comfort zone in that moment, she grew in faith and trust of God who saw her pain and her hurts. He met her in the midst of them.

What lessons of humility required to truly love have you learned from "Tale of Two Moms"? How will you respond differently to a current situation – or the next difficult one – in light of what you've learned?

Olive Oil Essence Droplets

*But I—I am like an olive tree flourishing in the House of God.
I trust in God's lovingkindness forever and ever.*
~Psalm 52:10 (TLV)

Fun Facts:

- The largest type of olive is known as a donkey olive, the smallest as a bullet olive.[19]

- The olive tree can live 2,000 years or more.[20]

- Olive trees can regenerate after fire.[20]

- The olive leaf symbolizes peace.[20]

- A single olive tree can produce up to 20 gallons of oil per year.[21]

- In ancient times in Israel olive oil was used for lighting, food, medicine, cosmetics, fuel.[21]

- Doors of ancient temple in Jerusalem were made of olive wood.[21]

- Eleven pounds of olives are required to produce one quart of olive oil.[22]

---

[19] http://www.softschools.com/facts/plants/olive_facts/539/ (Accessed 9/27/2018)
[20] http://m.jpost.com/PromoContent/The-Olive-in-the-Jewish-and-Israeli-culture-193416 (Accessed 9/27/2018)
[21] http://www.aish.com/jw/s/17-Amazing-Facts-about-Olives.html (Accessed 9/27/2018)
[22] http://weolive.com/about-olive-oils/fun-facts/ (Accessed 9/27/2018)

- On average the world consumes 2.25 million tons of olive oil each year.[22]

- During the 2004 Olympic Games in Athens, the old tradition of crowning Olympians with olive sprays was brought back to life. Over 2,550 olive branches were utilized to revive this tradition.[23]

Your Turn:

- Next time you're asked to bring an appetizer to share, try these cute fellows: Use black olives, carrots, and mozzarella balls to create penguin appetizers.[24]

- Try your hand at making olive bread. (This recipe is vegan.)[25]

- One of these appetizer recipes may become your new favorite: Cream Cheese Wrapped Olives[26] or Feta Cheese Wrapped Olives.[27]

- Many events in the Bible took place on the Mount of Olives. Olive wood is used to create beautiful nativity sets. Obtain one for your family or give as a gift – a reminder of the place Jesus met with His Father often, and where the Gospels show us one of His greatest moments of humility and love. He was born for that. They are available through many sources online and in stores.

- Cutting boards, dishes, spoons, knife blocks, artwork may all be made from olive wood. Do an internet or Pinterest search. Add an olive wood object to your home as a reminder of Jesus humility and love for us.

---

[23] http://weolive.com/about-olive-oils/fun-facts/ Accessed 9/27/2018)
[24] https://www.persnicketyplates.com/olive-penguins/ (Accessed 9/27/2018)
[25] https://www.macheesmo.com/olive-bread/ (Accessed 9/27/2018)
[26] https://bunnyswarmoven.net/cream-cheese-wrapped-olives/ (Accessed 9/27/2018)
[27] https://diethood.com/feta-cheese-covered-olives-giveaway/ (Accessed 9/27/2018)

Chapter 3

Flax
Humble Obedience

Cinnamah-Brosia and Friends Share About

Flax
Doing the Right Thing

Diffusing Today: Orange and Juniper
Aromatic Influence: May infuse a sense of peace, happiness, joy and spiritual awareness into the space
Daily Delight: Peanut Butter Energy Bites (featuring flax seeds and more)
Musically: **Audience of One** (Big Daddy Weave)
Verse of the Day:
> The one who has My commands and keeps them
> is the one who loves Me.
> And the one who loves Me will be loved by My Father.
> I also will love him and will reveal Myself to him."
> ~John 14:21

"Really?!" The girls' conversation burned in her ears and pained her heart. Kaitlyn met with these middle school girls for a year now at their request. A few of them found themselves in trouble. When they realized following the crowd proved a very unwise decision, two of them came to Kaitlyn and asked her to start a small group. They needed a safe place to share their hearts and struggles and receive encouragement to do the right thing.

Tonight they joined together to say "good-bye" to Taylor. Her family would be moving away in a few days. Cosmic Mountain, a games and eats place, offered a FREE "Ooey-Gooey Spectacular" dessert to celebrate a birthday. Always plenty to share, and the girls looked forward to birthday bashes at Cosmic Mountain.

Carson spoke up, "Hey we're going to miss the 'Ooey-Gooey Spectacular' with Taylor next month. Let's tell the server it's her birthday today, and have them bring one for her."

Ella agreed, "That's a great idea!"

Laney and Julia remained quiet. The expression on Taylor's face reflected the conflict she felt.

Carson carried on. "Come on Laney, Julia, what do you think? And Taylor you know you wouldn't want to miss your birthday treat!"

The prodding magnified Taylor's sad feelings right over the Cosmic Mountain moon. Already pained over missing her friends, this presented another reminder of her upcoming loss. The bonds formed over the past year bound these long-time friends together. The fun times, and the serious ones, and the "Ooey-Gooey Spectacular" ones all paraded themselves across her memory bank. She didn't want to miss the treat, but it wasn't her birthday either.

Laney and Julia decided the little lie was insignificant enough. They teamed up with Ella and Carson on this one. And it was decided — until Kaitlyn's loud exclamation hit their ears.

"You would do that? You would lie about Taylor's birthday just to get that dessert! You know God hates liars most of all. Remember last month you came to our meeting distraught over lies going around school about one of your classmates? We shared a lot of what God had to say about lying."

"But her birthday is just a few weeks away. It's not a big deal," Julia argued.

"We memorized some Bible verses about this, girls," Kaitlyn replied. "They apply to this situation."

> *Lying lips are detestable to the Lord, but faithful people are His delight.*
>
> ~Proverbs 12:22

> *Remember, it is sin to know what you ought to do and then not do it.*
>
> ~James 4:17 (NLT)

When the server passed their table again, Kaitlyn explained the situation. "The girls' friend, Taylor, is moving away in a few days. Her birthday is next month, and these friends are disappointed they will miss sharing the 'Ooey-Gooey Spectacular' with her. Would Cosmic Mountain make an exception?"

"Of course! We'll make your last night together special!"

Their server returned with the "Ooey-Gooey Spectacular" and six spoons. Several more employees followed him. The words of Cosmic Mountain's galactic birthday song rang out. They brought Taylor a t-shirt, and offered the group coupons for their next visit.

Kaitlyn smiled as they left thinking, "Thank You, God, for quick thinking to turn what could have been a horrible choice on the girls' part into a happy moment for them all." Taylor donned her t-shirt and the girls discussed their next trip to Cosmic Mountain without the guilt of having told a tall tale. The rewards for the truth are so much better!

The Essence of Flax in the Bible

A Humble Background Enhances Our Acts of Love

*Botanical Name: Linum usitatissimum;
all portions of the plant used for clothing, food, and more;
native to the Fertile Crescent (Iraq, Syria, Lebanon,
Cyprus, Jordan, Israel, Palestine, Egypt,
southeastern Turkey and western Iran)*

My grandmother knew fabrics. Many sought her accomplished skills with needle and thread. In her later years, my mom encouraged her to embroider tablecloth keepsakes for each of her five daughters and five granddaughters. Grandma worked on many of these during times she stayed at our home. That provided me a sneak peak.

Mom purchased the pre-stamped cloths and embroidery floss available in local department stores. As Grandma worked she taught me by sight and touch to recognize the finer linen fabrics. I chose a cloth done in shades of ecru and taupe. It baffled my mom why a teenager would choose something so colorless. I remember Grandma smiled and said, "I showed her the difference in the fabrics, and how this one is much nicer than the others."

Many years later counted-cross stitch gained popularity. My husband, a professional graphic artist, and I designed and published leaflets of cross-stitch patterns — many of the designs quite elaborate and stitched on linen. Naming the collection, I traveled straight back to the conversations with my grandmother. We made a play-on-words, combining my name and my love for linen and the colorful artistry of the butterfly to create "The Lynn'n Butterfly Collection." I loved color and butterflies, too, and their transformation from humble caterpillar to beautiful masterpiece!

When I chose the high-quality cloth and named the cross-stitch collection, the idea of linen's significance in the Bible never entered the picture. Is it ever significant!

I love the purity and simplicity of linen fabric. No fancy weave — just open and airy — it's color most often natural or ivory. Those characteristics give it a humble character, creating the perfect background to showcase cross-stitch and embroidery designs and skills.

God chooses linen for the wedding gown of the Bride of Christ. Look what it signifies.

> *Let us rejoice and shout for joy! Let us give Him glory and honor, for the marriage of the Lamb has come (at last), and His bride (the redeemed) has prepared herself. She has been permitted to dress in fine linen, dazzling white and clean — for the fine linen signifies the righteous acts of the saints (the ethical conduct, personal integrity, moral courage, and godly character of believers).*
>
> *Then the angel said to me, "Write, 'Blessed are those who are invited to the marriage supper of the lamb.'" And he said to me (further), "These are the true and exact words of God."*
>
> ~Revelation 19:8 (AMP)

Linen's purity and humbleness create the perfect backdrop for the righteous acts of Jesus' followers — His bride. Others observe the difference in our lives when we are in relationship with Jesus!

Integrity, moral courage, godly character, and ethical conduct stand out in our self-serving society. The beauty of a life lived like Jesus lived and loved stands out on its humble background — a beautiful masterpiece!

A Woman of the Bible Humble in Her Actions
Harlot Turned Heroine

*Hope begins in the dark,
the stubborn hope that if you just show up
and try to do the right thing, the dawn will come.
You wait and watch and work: you don't give up.*[28]
~Anne Lamott

We focused on Rahab in *The Essence of Joy* chapter on the joy of God's protection. This chapter on flax insisted we invite her back. Stretch you imagination with me as we engage in a bit of time travel. Give Rahab a big hug. Let's share a cup of coffee (or tea), and chat with this amazing woman.

Essence of Humility (EOH):
Good Morning, Rahab! Thanks for joining us. A fresh batch of cinnamon rolls just came out of the oven. They'll go great with our coffee.

Rahab: Oh, I would love one! And I'm excited to be here. Thank you for the invite. I admit a bit of culture shock, though. I'm observing everyone's clothes. So many different fabrics, and these do not appear hand made. Pardon me while I stare. We had linen and linen and more linen mostly. It's quite a tedious process to grow the flax and prepare it for spinning into fabric.

EOH: You were beginning the preparation part when the spies came to visit you in Jericho, right?

Rahab: We were. The stalks had been harvested. We arranged masses of them on the roof of the house to dry so we could separate the fibers from the stalks.

---

[28] https://www.brainyquote.com/quotes/anne_lamott_124535?src=t_do_the_right_thing (accessed 9/13/2018)

EOH: Before we talk more about the flax on the roof, can we back track a few moments and talk about your thoughts when the spies knocked on your door? I am a bit uncomfortable bringing this up, but the Bible tells us you were a harlot. Did you expect these particular men desired your services?

Rahab: That was my first thought, for sure! I quickly realized these were not locals, and they probably had a much different agenda at the moment. I knew they were some of those Israelites God blessed over the years. I was a young woman when they came. So, I was not alive 40 years earlier when it all happened, but the stories of God bringing them through the Red Sea lived on in our community as if it happened yesterday. The towns-people worried about them coming for us. Many of the men I entertained told the stories. Our families did, too. When these guys showed up we had just heard about what already became of the kings, Sihon and Og, and their lands. People in Jericho were terrified!

EOH: But you let them in, and you hid them? That was either really courageous or really stupid on your part. You knew your Jericho officials and your neighbors and friends would be furious if they knew you were with them. You protected them anyway. Why?

Rahab: (laughing) I'm often rather impulsive. My quick reactions frequently get me in some big trouble. That day was different. I'm not sure how I knew, but I knew: their God was the true God. Our people had lost all heart and courage when we learned their armies were approaching.

EOH: We are privileged to read your story in our Bible all these centuries later. So, we know you said these words to the spies:

> "I know the LORD has given you this land and that the terror of you has fallen on us, and everyone who lives in the land is panicking because of you."
>
> ~Joshua 2:9

How did you know this?

Rahab: Really, I can't explain it. But in that moment I became completely aware my only hope was in their God. I hid them in those flax stalks on the roof! Flax-drying season - what perfect timing!

EOH: How concerned were you when the king's men showed up at your door and inquired about those guys? Someone saw you talking to the men at your home. With your reputation, I'm sure that looked pretty bad for you.

Rahab: Yeah... I didn't really care about that. Everyone thought so poorly of me anyway unless they wanted "something" from me. My family loved me, but they were not happy about my profession. We all knew these Israelites would win. I had nothing to lose. I didn't even think twice. In my mind, my only hope was helping them!

EOH: And they promised you they would help! You and your family would be the only ones to escape when Jericho was destroyed. Right then you obeyed their instructions. You hung the scarlet cord out your window. And, wow! You quickly had a cover story! In hindsight, you know it was the Holy Spirit guiding you, I'm sure. But at the moment, did you even think anyone would believe the story you concocted? And sure enough, the city enforcers came knocking at your door with their questions about those men.

Rahab: I was a little scared, but it all just came to me so easily — where to hide the men, which escape route to tell them, and the story I gave the city officials about where to find the spies. I gathered up my family, and said, "Listen! We have to do exactly as these guys said. We are going to get out of this alive. Nobody else around here is. Are you with me?" To my surprise the whole family agreed. This all required a humbleness I didn't know I possessed. I turned down my "regular" business, and we waited. Maybe I was so trusting because those men respected me. That was a foreign experience to me. Mostly, I was just a commodity. You know when the Israelite army took Jericho — with the silliness of trumpets and shouts, I might add, my family was the only one saved. The Israelites took us into their camp and treated us like their family.

EOH: You married one of the Israelites, and your name is now recorded in the lineage of Jesus. You are King David's great-grandmother. Do you know your name is mentioned 3 times in the New Testament?

Rahab: Really? All I was doing is what I thought was the right thing at the time. I sure was glad I did, and it turned out to be the right thing — saved my whole family, you know. So, how exactly is my name included in the New Testament? Should I be worried?

EOH: (laughing just a little).... Well, it does say you were a harlot, but no worries.... you're honored to be one of only four women included in the genealogies of Jesus. I know you did the right thing! Here are the verses.

From Matthew's genealogy, and in James and Hebrews:

> *... and Salmon the father of Boaz by Rahab, and Boaz the father of Obed by Ruth, and Obed the father of Jesse,*
> ~Matthew 1:5 (RSV)

> *And in the same way was not also Rahab the harlot justified by works when she received the messengers and sent them out another way?*
> ~James 2:25 (RSV)

> *By faith Rahab the harlot did not perish with those who were disobedient, because she had given friendly welcome to the spies.*
> ~Hebrews 11:31 (RSV)

Rahab: I'm overwhelmed ... and humbled. I had no idea.

EOH: Since we have the New Testament now, there is another amazing hindsight fact I would like to share with you. As the Bride of Christ at the marriage supper of the Lamb, we will be wearing linen garments given to us by God representing our righteous acts.

> *"Let us rejoice and be glad and give the glory to Him, for the marriage of the Lamb has come and His bride has made herself ready." It was given to her to clothe herself in fine linen, bright and clean; for the fine linen is the righteous acts of the saints.*
>
> ~Rev 19:7-8

You covered the spies with the flax you dried to make into linen. And you "did the right thing." Our righteous acts in no way save us, but the Bible tells us often that Jesus' humble, loving, and sacrificial acts on our behalf provide our motivation to serve others. In another passage we have this reminder:

> *And our people must also learn to devote themselves to good works for cases of urgent need, so that they will not be unfruitful.*
>
> ~Titus 3:14

Your acts have blessed all of us through the centuries since you first invited those men to your rooftop shelter. The potential cost to you was enormous. Would you do it again?

Rahab: Absolutely! My best piece of encouragement for all generations — Do the right thing — the thing that you know in your heart God divinely directs you to do. I'll say it again. I really had nothing to lose. It might be a feeling or a little voice. It may be what you have learned from what you have witnessed or experienced. Or it may be what you know is God's voice even if you've never known Him before. He is always there. When we follow His prompts, we can be certain He's got the big picture. Look what He did with my life.

EOH: It strikes me, Rahab, that while you normally allowed men to pay you for carnal love that lacks everything, you offered the spies God's love, and God rewarded you for doing the right thing. What a beautiful story. Thank you so much for visiting with us today. Please stay and eat lunch with us.

Rahab's reputation boasted little integrity, yet her choice to act with compassion toward the spies was credited to her as righteousness. Her forgiveness and salvation stemmed from her trust in the One True God!

In what areas of your life have you chosen to do "the right thing" and seen God's hand at work? In what areas have you done "the right thing" and question why you are not seeing God's blessing?

God blessed her actions. He saved Rahab and her family. We look back on history and grasp the big picture God had in mind that day. Some blessings appear immediately. Others we may never witness in our lifetime. Pray for the big picture God is perfecting in your life and the life of your family – even many generations in the future.

Read the whole story of Rahab and the fall of Jericho in Joshua 2-6.

Flax Essence Droplets

She makes her own bedspreads.
She dresses in fine linen and purple gowns.
Her husband is well known at the city gates,
where he sits with the other civic leaders.
She makes belted linen garments
and sashes to sell to the merchants.
~Proverbs 31:22-24

Fun Facts:

- If you need an egg substitute, try tiny flax seeds. Here's how.[29]

- Flax sails were on all the great explorers' ships, as well as on those of Admiral Lord Nelson and Captain Cook.[30]

- The Jacquard mechanism used a system of punched cards to control the weaving of the pattern (on linen). This system of punched cards was later used by Charles Babbage and Herman Hollerith in calculating machinery and was an important step in the development of computers.[30]

- From the well-known works by the old masters to contemporary works of art, the most beautiful painters' canvases are made of linen.[30]

- "In 1855, as the price of paper rose, Dr. Deck proposed to dig up 2 1/2 million tons of Egyptian mummies, ship them to New York, unroll them; and use their linen wrappings to make paper."[30]

- Linen gets softer the more it is washed.[30]

---

[29] https://www.thekitchn.com/egg-substitutes-in-baking-try-95072 (Accessed 9/27/2018)
[30] https://www.fergusonsirishlinen.com/pages/index.asp?title2=Interesting-Facts&title1=About-Linen (Accessed 9/27/2018)

- Flax is a self-pollinating annual plant. From seed to harvest is approximately 100 days. The quality of flax is mainly determined by the characteristics of the root-end, length, thickness, and color of the stem.[30]

- Linen fabric wicks moisture and repels stains. It is also the perfect "green" fabric. The plants enrich the soil and every single part of the flax plant is used.[31]

- Flax seed, because of its reported health benefits, is part of the traditional cuisines of Asia, America, and Africa.[32]

Your Turn:

- Many of us have old linens from our mothers and grandmothers. This website offers clever ideas for repurposing them into new and useful items.[33]

- Create a spray to keep your dry linens fresh.[34]

- I mentioned loving to work counted cross-stitch projects on linen fabric. Learn more about techniques for doing this here.[35]

- Linen fabric is wonderfully elegant for napkins and placemats. They are available at many retailers and online, but you might enjoy making your own. Here is a very easy tutorial.[36]

---

[31] http://www.chicagonow.com/quilting-sewing-creating/2016/01/12-lively-facts-about-linen/ (Accessed 9/27/2018)
[32] https://www.organicfacts.net/health-benefits/seed-and-nut/health-benefits-of-flaxseed.html (Accessed 9/27/2018)
[33] http://www.elefantz.com/2014/11/ideas-for-using-vintage-linens.html Accessed 9/27/2018)
[34] https://wellnessmama.com/205948/linen-spray/ (Accessed 9/27/2018)
[35] https://www.needlework-tips-and-techniques.com/counted-cross-stitch.html (Accessed 9/27/2018)
[36] https://somuchbetterwithage.com/how-to-make-your-own-linen-napkins/ (Accessed 9/27/2018)

- Flaxseed is rich in omega 3s, potassium, oleic acids, and fiber. Mix your own superfood smoothies. Here's a recipe for a Blueberry Flax one.[37]

- Need ideas, in general, for cooking with flax seed, find ten recipes right here.[38]

---

[37] https://fitfoodiefinds.com/blueberry-flax-superfood-smoothie// (Accessed 9/27/2018)
[38] https://premeditatedleftovers.com/recipes-cooking-tips/10-great-flax-seed-recipes/ (Accessed 9/27/2018)

Chapter 4

Almond
Watchfulness and Promise

Cinnamah-Brosia and Friends Share About
Almond – Humility in Watchfulness

Diffusing Today: Ginger and Lime essential oils
Aromatic Influence: May help create a refreshed environment promoting courage and hopefulness
Daily Delight: Almond Cherry Bars
Musically: **Lead Me to You** (PJ Anderson)
Verse of the Day:
> Therefore, return to your God, Observe kindness and justice,
> And wait for your God continually.
> ~Hosea 12:6

"We all loved the shoe cutting party for Sole Hope and desired more service opportunities. The monthly Fish and Beans Night enthusiasm spilled over into our Ladies' group, too. I read these words of Jesus from Matthew's gospel this morning. They reminded me how important keeping our lights on and our eyes focused on the needs around us," Jane began one Tuesday evening.

> And you, beloved, are the light of the world. A city built on a hilltop cannot be hidden. Similarly it would be silly to light a lamp and then hide it under a bowl. When someone lights a lamp, she puts it on a table or a desk or a chair, and the light illumines the entire house. You are like that illuminating light. Let your light shine everywhere you go, that you may illumine creation, so men and women everywhere may see your good actions, may see creation at its fullest, may see your devotion to Me, and may turn and praise your Father in heaven because of it.
> ~Matthew 5:14-16 (Voice)

Crystal kept ideas coming. "Let's choose a Compassion® child to sponsor," she enthusiastically suggested to the ladies. "Their mission: 'Releasing children from poverty in Jesus' name.' We choose the country and the child. Sponsorship lasts as long as the child is in the program, usually 18-22 years old. Compassion® creates opportunities for sponsors to visit the children, too – a potential girls' trip and the perfect voyage to another place and culture. What do you think?"

We asked lots of questions about Compassion®. Crystal read this to us from their website:

> *It's a mission about love. We love God, and we demonstrate our love and live out our faith by extending care to others.*
>
> *We offer our programs to the poorest of the poor, to the children in greatest need, without ulterior motive. We devote ourselves to helping children of all faiths, cultures, backgrounds and race — without imposing any religious obligation or conversion requirement upon them.*
>
> *We simply aspire to be like our Savior, Jesus Christ, in who we are and what we do.*[39]

We explored the website, learned more, and chose to sponsor a child, but which one? We faced a tough decision? Crystal supplied packets of information for five adorable children in five different countries. We narrowed the decision to Toni, a 5-year old boy in Indonesia, and Daniela, an 8-year old girl in Nicaragua.

Nicaragua lies in relatively close proximity to the United States, making a trip there one day appear feasible, and an incredible trip for sure. The decision made, we turned to Crystal for the next step.

---

[39] https://www.compassion.com/mission-statement.htm (Accessed 9/27/2018)

Crystal explained about writing letters to Daniela. She furnished pretty paper, pens, and markers for us to begin. Haley wrote and decorated a favorite Scripture on her piece of paper to encourage Daniela:

> *Dear friends, let us love one another, because love is from God, and everyone who loves has been born of God and knows God.*
> ~1 John 4:7

Susan shared that one of her children had just accepted Jesus into his heart and how delighted she was. She included this Bible verse.

> *Let the little children come to Me. Don't stop them, for the kingdom of God belongs to such as these.*
> ~Mark 10:14

Crystal told her all about our little group of friends here at the Coffee Cottage who would be sponsoring her. She took pictures of everyone, which she would attach to the letters before mailing them.

Kaitlyn wrote how she and Gram worked together to make Miss Dot's Cafe into the Coffee Cottage where our friends and neighbors gather for coffee, treats, and most of all friendship and lots of Jesus.

At the end of the night, Crystal collected 10 wonderful "letters" to send to Daniela.

Daniela wrote to us, too. She sent news about her family and about her country. She described how they celebrated holidays, which foods were her favorites, and what she learned in her Compassion® center and in school.

Carol, more than the others, kept letters going to Daniela and kept a keen eye out for letter ideas. She announced one evening, "I have a new neighbor. Maggie moved here from Mexico. She's reading Daniela's letters with me, and helping me to come up with new things to share. Maggie translated a Bible verse into Spanish for me to put onto a piece of artwork I created for Daniela.

"Of course, Daniela's letters are already translated into English when we receive them, and our letters to her are translated into Spanish before they reach her hands. But I love doing this with Maggie. God gave me an opportunity to connect with a fellow sister-in-Christ, involve her in our ministry to Daniela, and invite her to join us on Tuesday evenings and for Fish & Beans nights. She is excited to meet others in our community. All of you are going to love her, too!" Carol pointed out.

Carol positions her spirit and heart to quickly perceive needs of those around her. She shares her faith and her love for Jesus with believers and unbelievers alike, recognizes Jesus when she sees Him in shoes, and she watches expectantly for Him. She watches just as intently for Him to return in glory. By His grace Jesus equipped each of us to do the same, and trusts we will. He tells us:

> "And the King will answer them, 'I assure you: Whatever you did for one of the least of these brothers of Mine, you did for Me.'"
>
> ~Matthew 25:40

Many options exist to reach out in love to the poor in our community and our world. How have you shown Jesus' love to those in need? Ministries to the homeless exist in many communities and are always in need of volunteers to shine Jesus' light. What about organizations helping refugees, or the local ministry focused on helping young women make life-affirming decisions when faced with unplanned pregnancies? You know of many more. In our culture controversy surrounds a few of these topics. People hold a broad spectrum of beliefs and convictions about them, but Jesus tells us to let our light shine. Every life needs Him!

Be encouraged to visit the Compassion® website.[40] Fall in love with one (or more) of the sweet faces, and become a sponsor, too. When you do, please remember to write regularly. The letters bring

---

[40] https://www.compassion.com/ (Accessed 9/27/2018)

big smiles and great encouragement to the children's hearts and lives. They treasure the letters more than you can imagine, because you took the time to personally shine Jesus' light into their world.

The Essence of Almond in Scripture

Jesus Instructs His Followers: "Watch!"

*Botanical Name: Prunus dulcis;
native to Mediterranean climate regions of the Middle East, from Syria and Turkey to India and Pakistan*

Almonds appear six times in the Old Testament, but receive zero mention in the New Testament. Our "Woman of the Bible" story will present us an up close look at almond in the Old Testament – a story filled with watchfulness. First, we learn Jesus spoke of watchfulness often.

He warned about false Messiahs and the signs of the last days:

> *Then Jesus began by telling them: "Watch out that no one deceives you. Many will come in My name, saying, 'I am He,' and they will deceive many. When you hear of wars and rumors of wars, don't be alarmed; these things must take place, but the end is not yet. For nation will rise up against nation, and kingdom against kingdom. There will be earthquakes in various places, and famines. These are the beginning of birth pains.*
>
> ~Mark 13:5-8

In the parable of the ten virgins, Jesus reminded us to always be alert and prepared because we do not know when He will return:

> *"Therefore be alert, because you don't know either the day or the hour."*
>
> ~Matthew 25:13

I encourage you to read the complete story of the ten virgins in Matthew 25:1-13

Again, in Luke 12 Jesus' warning revealed the ease of seduction by religious hypocrisy:

> "Be on your guard against the yeast of the Pharisees, which is hypocrisy. There is nothing covered that won't be uncovered, nothing hidden that won't be made known. Therefore, whatever you have said in the dark will be heard in the light, and what you have whispered in an ear in private rooms will be proclaimed on the housetops."
>
> ~Luke 12:1-3

In the same chapter Jesus presented yet another teaching on being alert and watchful, because greed can blind us to Him:

> "He then told them, "Watch out and be on guard against all greed because one's life is not in the abundance of his possessions." . . . "But God said to him, 'You fool! This very night your life is demanded of you. And the things you have prepared—whose will they be?' That's how it is with the one who stores up treasure for himself and is not rich toward God."
>
> ~Luke 12:20-21

Following Thursday evening's Passover meal with His disciples, Jesus knew the death He faced the next day, and He asked them to watch with Him for one hour while He prayed.

> *Then He came to the disciples and found them sleeping. He asked Peter, "So, couldn't you stay awake with Me one hour? Stay awake and pray, so that you won't enter into temptation. The spirit is willing, but the flesh is weak."*
>
> ~Matthew 26:40-41

Were Jesus' words etched on Peter's mind and heart when he wrote 1 Peter? He urged fellow believers to be watchful of the plots and strategies of the enemy:

> *Be serious! Be alert! Your adversary the Devil is prowling around like a roaring lion, looking for anyone he can devour.*
>
> ~1 Peter 5:8

To follow these instructions requires humility. How often we think "that won't happen to me," or "I've got plenty of time for Jesus another day," or "I'm really too tired or too busy to notice the person in need," or "this deadline is more important than worshipping with fellow believers today?" You know the scenarios. Our excuses sound a lot more like arrogance than humility. We miss the blessing.

The almond tree blooms before all the other flowers in Spring – a well-known symbol of Christ's resurrection! When we watch for the blossoms, we recognize His coming. Today. Tomorrow. Any day or hour.

He comes in the form of people in need, unlovable characters desperate for love, the downtrodden needing encouragement, the lonely seeking a hug and kind words. Discernment of the signs may alert us to an opportunity for inconvenience. What if we had been an inconvenience to Jesus?

Our humble attentiveness and love for others brings us closer to Him. We acknowledge His far greater sacrifice and take one step closer to Him. He is coming back again for those who watch and wait.

A Woman of the Bible Humble in Her Watchfulness

Samson's Mom: Humble Obedience in Her Watching and Waiting

Sometimes we wait for thunderclaps, drumrolls, and clarion calls to alert us to what's important when, actually, it's most often the subtle and persistent signals around us that make the most difference.[41]
~Martin Dempsey

When we plant the spring garden we anticipate the promise of a bountiful harvest to come. The harvest becomes a reality by watchful tending to deter weeds and critters. My grandfather attached aluminum pie plates to stakes in his garden. The noise generated by their movement in the breeze and the glare of sunshine bouncing from their faces served to keep bugs and varmints out. His attentiveness helped to ensure the harvest.

God promises so much to His children throughout Scripture. Mentioned in the previous devotion, we find six references to almonds in the Old Testament. Consider this one.

> *Then the Lord said to me, "Look, Jeremiah! What do you see?"*
> *And I replied, "I see a branch from an almond tree."*
> *And the Lord said, "That's right, and it means that I am watching, and I will certainly carry out all my plans."*
> ~Jeremiah 1:11-12

The Hebrew word for almond is "shakeid," rooted in a word that means to "watch" or to "wake." The Bible contains

---

[41] https://www.brainyquote.com/quotes/martin_dempsey_774599 (Accessed 9/27/2018)

many plays on words when we look to the deeper meaning of the Hebrew and Greek languages from which our English Bibles are translated. God asked Jeremiah what he had seen. I see a big smile on God's face and hear a chuckle as He tells Jeremiah it means, "I'm watching, and I'm delivering on my promises."

Samson's mom watched and waited. Remember Samson — the wild man in Judges 13-16? Even if you are familiar with the story, take the time to read these chapters. There's so much more to the story than most of us learned in our Sunday School lessons.

Samson's story started before his birth. God put Samson's mom to the test. Right here, I must stop and ask: How many of you moms out there lost your name to become "Jason's Mom" or "Heather's Mom" or "The Twins' Mom"? It happens all the time. The writer of his story called her "Samson's Mom" from the very start. We never learn her name!

We do learn her barrenness caused both Manoah and his wife great anguish. God heard their prayers and had big plans for their son.

> *Once again, though, the Israelites did evil according to the Eternal God, and He gave the Philistines power over them for 40 years. During that time, a man of Zorah named Manoah, from the tribe of Dan, was married to a wife who could bear him no children.*
>
> ***Messenger of the Eternal One*** *(appearing to Manoah's wife): You are barren and have no children, but all of that is about to change. You will conceive and have a son. Be careful that you don't drink wine or any other spirits (strong drink), and don't eat anything that is ritually impure, for you are going to become pregnant and have a son. Don't ever use a razor on his head, because you will raise this boy as a Nazirite, dedicated to the True God from his conception, and he will be the one to begin delivering Israel from the Philistines.*

> ***Manoah's Wife*** *(to her husband): A man of the True God visited me. He looked like a messenger of God, awe-inspiring. I didn't ask where he came from, and he didn't tell me his name, but he told me that I was going to become pregnant and bear a son. He told me not to drink wine or other spirits or to eat anything ritually unclean because our boy is to be a Nazirite, set apart for God from the day he is conceived until the day he dies.*
>
> ~Judges 13:1-7 (Voice)

The Visitor returned a second time to Samson's Mom. This time she ran back and invited Manoah to join her. Together they received the same message with the same instructions. In their joy they offered food to the Messenger. He instructed them to offer the grain to the Eternal. But when He declined their invitation to join them for a goat dinner, Manoah finally asked the question:

> Manoah had not realized that he was speaking to the Eternal's messenger. That is why he asked the Eternal's messenger a question.
>
> ***Manoah***: What is your name, so that we may honor you when your words become truth?
>
> ***Messenger of the Eternal One***: Why do you ask my name? It is incomprehensible, beyond human understanding.
>
> ~Judges 13:16-18 (Voice)
>
> ***Manoah*** (to his wife): We are most certainly going to die, for we have seen the True God!
>
> ~Judges 13:22 (Voice)

They fell on their faces in the presence of God, and Manoah expressed his fears. He remembered God's words to Moses many years earlier:

> *But He answered, "You cannot see My face, for no one can see Me and live."*
>
> ~Exodus 33:20

I believe Samson's Mom waited, watched, and pondered all these things she heard from the Messenger – just as Jesus' mother, Mary, pondered "all these things" many years later. In her heart Samson's Mom realized the message carried important implications. If either of them died now, how could a baby be born?

> **Manoah's Wife**: *If the Eternal had desired to kill us, then He would not have accepted the grain and burnt offerings from us or shown us these wonders or brought these announcements at this time.*
>
> *In due time, the woman did bear a son, and she named him Samson. The boy grew, the Eternal God blessed him, and the Spirit of the Eternal One began to move in him in Mahaneh-dan, between Zorah and Eshtaol.*
>
> ~Judges 13:23-25 (Voice)

Samson's parents followed the instructions they had been given. Rather than an inconvenience, I believe they recognized an opportunity to live a worshipful life. Samson kept the Nazirite vows, too. He also made many questionable choices through the years and acted nearly as bad or worse than the heathens they lived among. One infamous incident related to Delilah and her manipulative powers over him looked like his demise. In the end he accepted the responsibility for his actions and cried out to God:

Samson *(crying out to the Lord): Lord, Eternal One, remember me and fill me with strength this one last time, O True God, so that with this last act of revenge I can pay back the Philistines for the loss of my sight.*

He took hold of the two main pillars of the building, the ones supporting the roof, and he leaned hard against them, his right hand on one, his left hand on the other.

Samson: *Let me die here with the Philistines.*

He pushed with all his might. The pillars gave; the building collapsed on the rulers and all the Philistine people who were in it. The number of enemies that he killed at his death was greater than the number of Philistines he had killed during the rest of his life.

Then his brothers and the rest of his family came down from the hill country and took his body back up to be buried between the towns of Zorah and Eshtaol in the burial ground of his father Manoah. Samson had been judge of Israel for 20 years.

~Judges 16:28-31 (Voice)

No, we never learned her name. – simply Samson's mom. Like moms do, she committed to do everything possible for her child. She followed the commands of the Eternal One. If you read the story (Judges 13-16) you know Samson's actions caused his parents heartache. In the end He honored the Nazirite vows and God.

Since she is not mentioned at the end of the story, it is believed God sparred her the witness of the last scene of her son's life – pain enough to crush every mom's heart. If present, her mom-pride would have glowed beyond her pain as she realized up close and personal the redemption and restoration God offers to all of us. God loved Samson, and Samson's Mom – tremendously! When he served and saved his countrymen from the Philistines in a final display of the strength God had given him, Samson delivered on the good work that our Heavenly Father prepared in advance for Him to do.

Samson's Mom watched and waited with love and commitment to the Eternal One. God loved her so much. She became the only woman in the Old Testament who saw God!

> Do you wonder what a Nazirite is?
> *(Heb. form Nazirite), the name of such Israelites as took on them the vow prescribed in Numbers 6:2-21. The word denotes generally one who is separated from others and consecrated to God. Although there is no mention of any Nazirite before Samson, yet it is evident that they existed before the time of Moses. The vow of a Nazirite involved these three things, (1) abstinence from wine and strong drink, (2) refraining from cutting the hair off the head during the whole period of the continuance of the vow, and (3) the avoidance of contact with the dead.*[42]

---

[42] https://www.biblestudytools.com/dictionaries/eastons-bible-dictionary/nazarite.html (Accessed 9/17/2018)

Almond Essence Droplets

But I will look to the LORD;
I will wait for the God of my salvation.
My God will hear me.
~Micah 7:7

Fun Facts:

- Almonds are 100% reliant on wild bees and honey bees for crop pollination — no bees, no almonds.[43]

- Almonds are a member the rose family and are often called "the queen of the rose family." The fuzzy hull around the almond nut feels kind of like a peach. Other family members of the almond are the peach and the apricot.[43]

- Almonds were a prized ingredient in bread served to Egypt's Pharaohs.[44]

- Almond trees live 20-25 years. They do not produce fruit during the first 3-4 years.[44]

- 40% of the world's almonds are used by chocolate makers.[44]

- Because the almond tree is the first fruit tree to flower in the lands of the Bible, it is a well-known symbol of resurrection.[45]

---

[43] https://www.foodconfidence.com/2013/09/18/eat-almonds/ (Accessed 9/27/2018)
[44] http://justfunfacts.com/interesting-facts-about-almonds/ (Accessed 9/27/2018)
[45] Lytton John Musselman, *Figs, Dates, Laurel, and Myrrh: Plants of the Bible and the Quran*, Portland, Oregon: Timber Press, 2007.

Your Turn:

- *You might imagine, most of the ways to use almonds are in foods. You'll definitely find a few recipes in this list, along with a couple other fun ideas!*[44]

- *Almond is not an essential oil, it is a fatty oil, but almond smells heavenly (at least in my humble opinion). Here's an option for Vanilla Almond Sugar Scrub.*[46]

- *Make Rose Almond Body Oil for a refreshing after-shower treat for your skin.*[47]

- *Chewy Italian Amaretti Almond Cookies grabbed my attention as a must try for the holidays (or any day).*[48]

- *Do you love bananas and chocolate together? This Double-Chocolate Banana Bread Recipe uses almond flour.*[49]

- *We've learned that 40% of the world's almonds are used by chocolate makers. Join in the fun by making Almond Truffles. These have a chocolate almond fudge center and are covered in white chocolate.*[50]

---

[46] http://thecountrymitten.com/2018/04/22/diy-vanilla-almond-sugar-scrub/ (Accessed 9/27/2018)
[47] https://helloglow.co/diy-rose-almond-body-oil-more-uses-for-wilting-roses/ (Accessed 9/27/2018)
[48] https://www.mangiabedda.com/chewy-amaretti-italian-almond-cookies/ (Accessed 9/27/2018)
[49] http://thetoastedpinenut.com/double-chocolate-banana-bread/ (Accessed 9/27/2018)
[50] https://www.shugarysweets.com/almond-truffles/ (Accessed 9/27/2018)

- Candied almonds are a popular snack. This version may become your new favorite. Smoky Sweet Spiced Almonds.[51]

---

[51] http://www.rockrecipes.com/smoky-sweet-spiced-almonds/ (Accessed 9/27/2018)

Chapter 5

Chamomile
Trust The Word

Cinnamah-Brosia and Friends Share About
Chamomile
Humbly Trusting "The Word"

Diffusing Today: Chamomile
Aromatic Influence: Helps create and atmosphere of peace and patience
Daily Delight: Lemon Chamomile Shortbread Cookies
Musically: **Beautiful Savior** (Traditional Hymn)
Verse of the Day:
> *Some trust in chariots and some in horses,*
> *but we trust in the name of the Lord our God.*
> ~~Psalm 20:7 (NIV)

(Cinnamah-Brosia narrates the stories at her Coffee Cottage. This one is an exception. In a fun twist, the author of the book [Lynn, of course] narrates the story. Previous stories at the Coffee Cottage are those of her friends. No friends brought the author a story to include here. Lynn visits the Coffee Cottage and shares one of her own. Lynn is the narrator for this one.)

"Oh to have a photo of the priceless look of surprise on Cinnamah-Brosia's face when she saw me at the door. It's not often the author of your fictional world shows up in your fictional Coffee Cottage, but that's exactly what I did today."

"Lynn, what are you doing here?" Cinnamah-Brosia asked. "We may seem real to you, but you know you made us up. As long as you're here, though, join Jane and I over in Wisdom Corner. Here's a cup of your favorite coffee and a few lemon chamomile shortbread cookies. I can't wait to hear the story that prompted your visit!"

"Your friends haven't come through with a story to fit the chamomile chapter. Chamomile encourages an atmosphere of peace and patience. So, does completely trusting the Word of God — and trusting The Word – best known as Jesus. It all reminded me of one of my own experiences. May I share?"

"You're writing the book — hardly think we can object," Jane responded with a few added giggles.

"Great! First of all remember Crystal suggested you make a girls' trip to visit your group's Compassion® child? This story happened on a trip like that.

"Our group of ladies traveled to El Salvador with Compassion®. I must say, 'I don't believe a gallon of chamomile would have calmed some of the nerves on the bus that day.' Excited to learn more about Compassion®, meet our sponsored children, and share ministry and fellowship, our group of 30+ ladies along with local group leaders and translators boarded a large touring bus at the airport in San Salvador. This country celebrated its independence in mighty big ways, and this was the week.

"We were awed by the site of a large group of people dressed in traditional attire moving through the street. A man in a white suit with a large white hat and a woman in a flowing white gown seemed to guide the group from the back — or maybe they followed to see where the younger folks would lead this frivolity. Not only was it magnificent to behold, it caused a major detour around the town and beyond to arrive at our destination. Their Independence Day remained a few days off. This may have been a pop-up celebration. Scheduled or not, the street party received the right-of-way.

"Police escorted us. The bus proceeded onto narrower and narrower roads as we rerouted to our destination. Someone designed these roads for two tiny cars, I'm certain, to wonder how they would pass when they met up. On one side of the bus the hills rose. The other side presented a sheer drop down the side of the mountain. Rocks and ruts cluttered our path. The bus rocked, bounced, and otherwise jangled. Nerves jangled, too! Many reasons existed for fear and worry. If the bus failed to make it through, great chance existed it could be at the bottom of that mountain along with the driver and all the passengers.

"Police and others along the way manually cleared rocks and debris from our path attempting to offer the driver a bit more space to maneuver. Eventually conditions required the driver to turn the bus around in an even tighter spot.

"While grateful for the driver's amazing skills behind the wheel, the police, and anyone who helped to clear our way, it became crystal clear the real trust was in God alone. I don't remember the verses our leaders shared that day. I don't remember the words of their prayers, but we joined together and humbly declared to God our lives were truly in His hands. He could deliver us. We prayed to trust He would.

"I experienced a most surreal feeling of knowing He traveled on the bus with us. If we went down the side of the mountain, He would be there before we were. If we made it through He was already at our destination to raise shouts of joy with us and to receive our thanks and praise. My sense of peace defied explanation. The incident served as a powerful reminder of the power of the Word of God and of His Son, The Word, come to live among us, die for us, and assure us of being with Him forever. The peace from breathing in the aromas of His creation — like chamomile or lavender — offers reminders of the ultimate peace He came to bring even in the most harrowing of circumstances.

"Most of us in the group met each other for the first time that day. Together we survived the ordeal, and an amazing week of ministry followed – ministry to others and ministry to each other. Humbled describes our lives when those we came to serve ministered to us in ways we never imagined.

"Our group remains close today – three years later – loving one another, cheering each other on, crying on one another's shoulder, and always giving glory to God for His indescribable love – The Word made flesh and living among us and in us."

Lynn finished. Jane and C-B remained quiet for a moment. C-B responded: "I'm visualizing my self in the situation and hope I would have experienced that same peace." Jane nodded in agreement before she spoke.

"Lynn, two Scriptures came to my mind as you related your story to us. Did you think of them then, too?"

So be strong and courageous! Do not be afraid and do not panic before them. For the Lord your God will personally go ahead of you. He will neither fail you nor abandon you.
~Deuteronomy 31:6 (NLT)

And remember, I am with you always, to the end of the age.
~Matthew 28:20

"Those are great words from our God. I love that Jesus is The Word and He gifted us with many words for just the right moment. Yes, our thoughts lingered on those verses and others like them," I replied.

"Hey, on another note – I brought you girls a gift. You giggled about me asking to share my story at the Coffee Cottage, because I made you up in the first place. Well, our cover artist created paper dolls to look like you, Cinnamah-Brosia. They are on the next page for our readers, too."

"Jane, C-B, and I reveled in a hearty laugh. We do hope you enjoy them as much as our artist did creating them."

NOTE: We suggest you copy these from the paperback book or print from your ebook. Printing the doll on index card weight paper, or printing on regular paper and pasting to light weight cardboard is suggested. Print the clothes on regular weight paper.

Cinnamah-Brosia paper doll and doll clothes are ©Copyright (2018): Lynn U. Watson. Permission is granted to copy these for your personal or small group use.

The Essence of Chamomile in Scripture

We May be Blown Away Like the Flowers of the Field, But God's Word Stands Forever

*Botanical Name: M. chamomilla
is the most popular source of the herbal product chamomile;
an annual plant of the composite family Asteraceae.
Native to: North Africa, Europe, and temperate regions of Asia;
essential oil is steam distilled from flowers;*

When I titled this third volume in Cinnamah-Brosia's Coffee Cottage series **The Essence of Humility**, I believed it important to feature commonly known and used botanicals, fruits, and oils. I envisioned the humble daisy-like blossoms of the chamomile plant as the perfect backdrop for the cover. C-B and her friends sit in a field of them.

Commentaries mention chamomile as the probable "flowers of the field" referred to in Isaiah 40. The prophet Isaiah contrasted the fleeting nature of the flowers with the Word of God that stands forever.

> *Listen! It's the voice of someone shouting, "Clear the way through the wilderness for the Lord! Make a straight highway through the wasteland for our God! Fill in the valleys, and level the mountains and hills. Straighten the curves, and smooth out the rough places. Then the glory of the Lord will be revealed, and all people will see it together. The Lord has spoken!"*
>
> *A voice said, "Shout!"*
> *I asked, "What should I shout?"*

> "Shout that people are like the grass. Their beauty fades as quickly as the flowers in a field. The grass withers and the flowers fade beneath the breath of the Lord. And so it is with people. The grass withers and the flowers fade, but the word of our God stands forever."
>
> ~Isaiah 40: 3-8 (NLT)

From the pen of Jesus' beloved disciple, John, we read:

> *In the beginning was the Word, and the Word was with God, and the Word was God. He was with God in the beginning. All things were created through Him, and apart from Him not one thing was created that has been created. Life was in Him, and that life was the light of men. That light shines in the darkness, yet the darkness did not overcome it.*
>
> ~John 1:1-5

John's declaration: "The Word is Jesus. He stands forever." To live and love like He does, we recognize our short time on earth, and acknowledge our opportunity to allow His light to shine through us like flowers, which bring joy for a season.

Aromatically, chamomile is believed to help eliminate the emotional charge of irritability and nervousness, to help stabilize emotions, and to help soothe and clear the mind, creating an atmosphere of peace and patience. When we reach for a cup of chamomile tea at the end of the day or soothe our tired baby with lotion infused with chamomile, we expect those benefits.

Such experiences remind me of the lingering presence of Jesus, The Word, which transforms our lives to reflect His love. In whatever circumstance we find ourselves, we rest assured as Christ followers, His light shines far brighter than our frail ability to face life's challenges without Him.

> *For once you were full of darkness, but now you have light from the Lord. So live as people of light!*
>
> ~Ephesians 5:8 (NLT)

I don't tolerate "inefficient" and "stupid" well. In my silly little flower-life, I sometimes allow aggravation toward behavior I consider "stupid" to manifest in most inappropriate ways.

I remember a particular day when a co-worker in the space of just a few minutes time, crossed all my boundaries. How often I would have exploded! Without my realization at the moment, The Word that stands forever controlled my reactions. The co-worker finally took a breath — my opportunity to respond. Burning on the inside I simply said with what I perceived to be a not-so-kind tone of voice, "Are you done?" I presumed my body language and facial expression projected much less than kindness or humility.

In my eyes, I reacted terribly. A manager who witnessed the interplay questioned me at the end of the incident. "How did you do that? You didn't let it get to you at all. You handled it so well, and everyone's jets are cooled."

On the inside I withered like flowers in the grass. My response to her question fumbled from my mouth. "I didn't realize I did anything unusual. From my viewpoint I handled it poorly. If you saw something different, it was a God thing."

The manager was not a believer, but she saw the light of Jesus shining through what I deemed a failure. Did I love like Jesus on that day better than I thought? Perhaps. For sure, He works in spite of our weaknesses.

My stinky flesh did not earn the manager's response to the power of those words. My Jesus, The Word, alone provided her that glimpse of His glory. I was humbled. She perceived something different than the wilting flower of my flesh.

When flowers wilt they release seeds. Years later I look back and realize the seeds of my simple words offered her an opportunity to witness the power of "The Word."

Rather than laugh at my humble confession, I believe she pictured the beauty of God in the flower as it wilted and released a seed of His glory. The seed implanted in her heart. Did it make a forever difference for the manager that day? I pray it did.

A Woman of the Bible Humble in Her Trusting
If Only She Could Touch the Hem of His Garment

When you take a flower in your hand and really look at it,
it's your world for the moment.
I want to give that world to someone else.
Most people in the city rush around so,
they have no time to look at a flower.
I want them to see it whether they want to or not.[52]
~~Georgia O'Keeffe

We make a request of Jesus. We watch Him help others and question, "Will He come to my rescue or not?" What faces do our questions wear among the people we encounter? Do we see our problems as more significant than someone else's, or do we see ourselves unworthy of Jesus touch? Are we joyous and amazed for miracles that happen in others' lives? Do we realize we can be a part of those miracles when we get our eyes off of self? When we look, watch, and trust, He guides us to notice the needs of others. Often our own healing comes in the serving.

Jesus always looked and watched to see what His Father was doing. In the case of this woman, however, He wasn't even aware of her. She told herself, "If I just touch the hem of His garment, all these troubles will go away." This woman suffered for twelve years with bleeding problems. Doctors took all her money with no positive results to show for it. Healthcare must have been costly then, too.

Those in the crowd who knew her condition, judged themselves and Jesus unclean from brushing against her. Jewish laws forbid the unclean to enter the temple. Did she remember God's word of promise from the Old Testament?

---

[52] https://www.brainyquote.com/quotes/georgia_okeeffe_138692 (Accessed 9/27/2018)

> *But for you who fear My name, the sun of righteousness will rise with healing in its wings, and you will go out and playfully jump like calves from the stall.*
>
> ~Malachi 4:2

Jesus, The Word, taught us how to apply the "Word." There are healing and blessings in His wings (the hem of His garment). They bring us closer to God when we obey His law written on our hearts.

> *Look, the days are coming when I will bring about a new covenant with the people of Israel and Judah. It will not be like the covenant I made with their ancestors long ago when I took them by the hand and led them out of slavery in Egypt. They did not remain faithful to that covenant—even though I loved and cared for them as a husband. This is the kind of new covenant I will make with the people of Israel when those days are over. I will put My law within them. I will write it on their hearts. I will be their God, and they will be My people. No longer will people have to teach each other or encourage their family members and say, "You must know the Eternal." For all of them will know Me intimately themselves—from the least to the greatest of society. I will be merciful when they fail and forgive their wrongs. I will never call to mind or mention their sins again.*
>
> ~Jeremiah 31:31-34 (Voice)

The woman worked her way through the crowd and finally positioned herself close enough to touch the hem — just the very edge — of His robe. Jesus didn't shun her. He didn't screw up His face at her. Jesus asked, "Who touched Me?"

We almost hear the disciples' laughter at such a question. "All these people and you ask who touched You? Come on, Jesus! Lots of people did."

This one woman, though, touched Him with great intention. He felt power leave Him. He needed to get a message to the woman with faith and determination to approach Him.

Did she come forward with timidity to share her whole story? Did she declare a bunch of apologies for being unclean? What expectations prompted her actions? Did she feel bathed in the kindness of His words when Jesus asked who touched Him? Did she respond with reverent awe and amazement, when she realized He even knew she had? That answer remains a mystery, but we know Jesus' response:

> *"Daughter," He said to her, "your faith has made you well. Go in peace and be free from your affliction."*
> ~~Mark 5:34

Be sure, she welcomed her healing with excitement. And in the healing she was also made clean — no longer plagued by the stigma of the Jewish laws. Shout Hallelujah!

We can come to Him anytime without fear of being condemned or seen as unclean. He welcomes us, and He scrubs us up! The cleansing is not always physical, but every time it is spiritual! He makes us new creations by the power of His words over us. We discover and cherish His words every time we spend time with The Word. That happens when we read and study His word, the Bible. The Word of God contains all the words of The Word.

Spending time with The Word, we learn to trust Him more deeply, and He encourages us to lift others struggling with pain and condemnation, leading them to His healing powers, too.

> *He always comes alongside us to comfort us in every suffering so that we can come alongside those who are in any painful trial. We can bring them this same comfort that God has poured out upon us.*
> ~2 Corinthians 1:4 (TPT)

Be encouraged to find a Bible translation you love, and spend time with The Word each day. If you do not own a Bible, visit Bible Gateway (https://biblegateway.com). Bible Gateway allows you to read many versions of the Bible for free.

(NOTE: The Hebrew word for "wings" in Malachi 4:2 is the same word used for the "tassels" on the hems of the rabbis' garments. When the woman reached for the hem of Jesus' robe, she acknowledged the Malachi verse and trusted for the "healing in His wings."

Chamomile Essence Droplets

Awaken, north wind — come, south wind.
Blow on my garden and spread the fragrance of its spices.
Let my love come to his garden and eat its choicest fruits.
~Song of Solomon 4:16

Fun Facts:

- Chamomile is one of the oldest of all herbs, dating back to ancient Egyptians. It is both a pretty flower and an ancient healer.[53]

- Chamomile is in the same flower family as asters and daisies. It is the national flower of Russia.[54]

- Chamomile is probably the most widely used relaxing herb in the world.[55]

- The fresh chamomile plant has the scent of apples.[55]

- Chamomile tea is made from dried chamomile flowers.[56]

Your Turn:

- Try Sleepy Time Tea Recipe featuring chamomile.[57]

---

[53] https://www.dermascope.com/scope-this/some-interesting-facts-about-chamomile-february-2011 (Accessed 9/27/2018)
[54] https://www.zokiva.com/blogs/news/8-interesting-facts-about-chamomile-tea (Accesed 9/27/2018)
[55] https://www.theflowerexpert.com/content/giftflowers/flowersandfragrances/chamomile (Accessed 9/27/2018)
[56] https://en.m.wikipedia.org/wiki/Chamomile (Accessed 9/27/2018)
[57] https://carolynharrington.com/food-as-medicine/tea-recipe-for-sleep/ (Accessed 9/27/2018)

- Great Gift Idea: Handmade Lavender Chamomile Tea Soap. Here are the directions.[58]

- Wow! This site has 23 ways to use chamomile. You're sure to find one you'll love.[59]

---

[58] https://apumpkinandaprincess.com/lavender-chamomile-tea-soap/ (Accessed 9/27/2018)
[59] https://theherbalacademy.com/23-ways-to-use-chamomile/?ap_id=growagoodlife (Accessed 9/27/2018)

Chapter 6

Eucalyptus Restoration and Promises Delivered

Cinnamah-Brosia and Friends Share About
Eucalyptus
Loving In Spite of...

Diffusing Today: Eucalyptus and Lemon
Aromatic Influence: May help to promote well being; and may help to purify the air
Daily Delight: Lemon Bars
Musically: **Breathe** (Michael W. Smith)
Verse of the Day:

> *He renews my strength.*
> *He guides me along right paths,*
> *bringing honor to his name.*
> **~(Psalm 23:3, NLT)**

Carol announced her mom, Miss Alice, planned to be in Pearlville next week. Miss Alice and Gram had shared a great friendship. Miss Alice loved to tell her stories. We missed her when she and Mike moved away. We eagerly anticipated her visit.

A typical Monday morning brings a brisk flow of customers in and out of the Coffee Cottage. When Carol and Miss Alice came through the door, I lifted a quick prayer of thanks that this was not one of those mornings. Jane and I knew Carol and Miss Alice's orders by heart. We prepared their plates and beverages, and we included lemon bars, too. They claimed the "Special of the Day" title today. And Miss Alice is special.

Jane said, "Oh, please share one of your stories with everyone enjoying their coffee this morning."

Miss Alice jumped right in, of course. She often repeated her stories, but if we heard this one before, we listened again anyway.

"I met Mike at college. He came from a small country town. I was a city girl. We were so different. It was love at first sight."

"Mike was his mother, Agnes', pride and joy. From the first time we met, she didn't like me. I was the enemy. The feeling was mutual.

"I learned later, she set her sights on a hometown girl she hoped Mike would marry — a girl he knew all his life. Agnes planned for him to finish college, return home, marry and live near her. I was not in her plans.

"She reminded Mike often to honor his father and his mother — always with Bible verses. She quoted his one more than any other for obvious reasons.

> *Honor your father and your mother so that you may have a long life in the land that the Lord your God is giving you.*
>
> ~Exodus 20:12

"We quickly tired of her insistence to have it her way. Mike and I married three months after meeting. She resented me and announced to all her friends how unacceptable her daughter-in-law was. The feeling mutual, I hardened my heart against her.

"Vietnam came along, and her worst nightmare came true. Mike was drafted, quit college and served his country. His mom continued her aggressive behavior toward me.

"The thing was, we both loved Mike. As the war went on I saw her fear. I put aside my feelings to comfort her. That was one of the hardest things I ever did. She still held me at arms length, and showed hostility at my efforts.

"When Mike returned home, we started a family, and our life took us on a path, which led away from Agnes. "When we moved to Pearlville our lives were messy. We loved each other, but his mom's continuous rejection of my kindnesses made me question if Mike and I should be together.

"All the interference from his mom drove Mike and I away from the church. Miss Dot and I became fast friends. She loved on me in spite of all my misgivings and shortcomings. I whined to her constantly. She always had just the right Bible verses to encourage me to keep treating Mike's mom with love and respect no matter how she reacted. Miss Dot kept saying God has a plan for this, and quoting these verses over and over:

Trust in the Lord with all your heart, and do not rely on your own understanding; think about Him in all your ways, and He will guide you on the right paths.
~Proverbs 3:56

"For I know the plans I have for you" — this is the Lord's declaration —"plans for your welfare, not for disaster, to give you a future and a hope".
~Jeremiah 29:11

"Agnes grew older. When she became ill, she turned to me for help. We both swallowed our pride. Through God's grace we became friends."

Miss Alice had not shared this story before. After a few thoughtful moments Jane looked Miss Alice in the eyes and said, "That took constant reminders to self to be humble, I'm sure, Miss Alice. What a tough assignment. It's easy to seek retaliation against people treating us like Agnes treated you. You probably thought of some mean things to torment her instead of showing her kindness. This story shows your humility and God delivered on His promise to honor your trust in Him. Like a breath of fresh air, your relationship with your mother-in-law transformed. Lynn is writing another book. Would it be okay if she shared it?"

"Of course! What an honor – and oh my – another opportunity to be humble."

"And the title of this one is The Essence of Humility," Cinnamah-Brosia chimed in.

The Essence of Eucalyptus (Myrtle) in the Bible
Breathe in Love

*Botanical Name: Myrtis communis;
native to Mediterranean area;
oil steam-distilled from the leaves*

When plagued with a stuffy nose or congestion, do you reach for eucalyptus? This is one aromatherapy fragrance most everyone knows. It makes its appearance in this volume of *Cinnamah-Brosia's Inspirational Collection* focusing on more commonly known and loved botanicals, which are also found in Scripture.

If you believe the Bible contains no eucalyptus, this chapter poses a challenge. God's awesomeness amazes me all the time. I prayed, and He led me right to His solution.

All eucalyptus is in the myrtle family. When we reach for eucalyptus or another product that includes it in the ingredient list we expect we may breathe more easily assisted by its aroma.

While eucalyptus remains absent, myrtle appears several times in the Bible.

The lulav, integral to the Feast of Tabernacles (Sukkot), includes myrtle. To fill the requirement for Sukkot, three leaves must grow from one point on the myrtle stem. For the Jews, myrtle can symbolize sweetness, justice, divine generosity, peace, God's promise, and recovery.[60]

> *On the first day you are to take the product of majestic trees—palm fronds, boughs of leafy trees, and willows of the brook—and rejoice before the Lord your God for seven days.*
>
> ~Leviticus 23:40

---

[60] https://godasagardener.com/2012/12/16/zechariah-and-the-myrtle-tree-2/ (Accessed 9/27/2018)

Numerous commentaries agree boughs of leafy trees are myrtle. Later in Nehemiah, when he directs the people to celebrate the long-forgotten feast again, they gather myrtle.

> *So they proclaimed and spread this news throughout their towns and in Jerusalem, saying, "Go out to the hill country and bring back branches of olive, wild olive, myrtle, palm, and other leafy trees to make booths, just as it is written."*
> ~Nehemiah 8:15

Zechariah witnessed visions and received instructions from the Angel of the Lord standing among myrtle trees.

> *I looked out in the night and saw a man riding on a red horse. He was standing among the myrtle trees in the valley. Behind him were red, sorrel, and white horses. I asked, "What are these, my lord?"*
>
> *The angel who was talking to me replied, "I will show you what they are."*
>
> *Then the man standing among the myrtle trees explained, "They are the ones the LORD has sent to patrol the earth."*
>
> *They reported to the Angel of the LORD standing among the myrtle trees, "We have patrolled the earth, and right now the whole earth is calm and quiet."*
> ~Zechariah 1:8-11

How many times have you heard deep breathing helps keep us grounded? Right there among the myrtle/eucalyptus trees the whole earth rested in peace. I imagine the prophet breathed deeply in the presence of the Lord.

Following His resurrection Jesus' appeared to His followers. He brought His word of peace to them. He took a deep breath and breathed into them, too.

> The disciples, seeing the Master with their own eyes, were exuberant. Jesus repeated his greeting: "Peace to you. Just as the Father sent me, I send you."
>
> Then he took a deep breath and breathed into them. "Receive the Holy Spirit," he said.
> ~John 20:20-22a

In Creation the Father breathed the breath of life into Adam. Jesus breathed new life – the presence of the Holy Spirit – into His friends' lives. Did the fragrance of eucalyptus hang in the air?

God's Spirit in us empowers us to live and love like Jesus. Jesus words served as a reminder of a verse from the book of Micah.

> But me—I'm filled with God's power, filled with God's Spirit of justice and strength,
> ~Micah 3:8a (MSG)

Jesus breathes new life into us, too. Allow the aroma of eucalyptus to serve as a reminder of the Spirit's presence in your life. It comes with the promise of restoration and peace in the presence of God. Spread its fragrance all around!

A Woman of the Bible Humbly Believes

Myrtle Instead of Nettles

Let each man think himself an act of God,
His mind a thought, his life a breath of God;
And let each try, by great thoughts and good deeds,
To show the most of Heaven he hath in him.[61]
~Philip James Bailey

A family member recently remarked, "I've often thought I should make a Monopoly board of all the places Grace and Erv lived." Grace and Erv are my mom and dad. After she mentioned this, I purposed to list every single place they/we lived. My list included 30+ different addresses from the time they married until my mom passed (1947-2001). I attended 16 different schools between Kindergarten and High School graduation — a few times I attended three different schools in one school year.

Our moves stemmed from poor choices my dad made over the years. He also made many impossible-to-keep promises each time. Amidst the pain and tears, the moves required substantial amounts of humble submission on my mom's part.

Abram received directions from God to move his family to a whole new land far from everyone and everything they knew. No evidence is recorded that Sarai argued with Abram about these moves. Her decision to follow required at least as much humility as my mom's decisions did — probably more. Mom always knew something about the place we were going next, and sometimes a few family members lived nearby. Sarai went along, knowing nothing of the challenges ahead. Along their journey Abram and Sarai both made poor choices. Let's call those poor choices nettles.

---

[61] https://quotefancy.com/quote/1078464/Philip-James-Bailey-Let-each-man-think-himself-an-act-of-God-His-mind-a-thought-his-life (Accessed 9/27/2018)

> *Where once there were thorns, cypress trees will grow. Where nettles grew, myrtles will sprout up. These events will bring great honor to the LORD's name; they will be an everlasting sign of his power and love."*
> ~Isaiah 55:13 (NLT)

The *The Merriam-Webster Dictionary* defines nettles as "any of a genus (Urtica of the family Urticaceae, the nettle family) of chiefly coarse herbs armed with stinging hairs"[62]

Sarai and Abram both made poor choices. (Genesis 12-25 covers their full story. For a more complete understanding, take the time to read those chapters.) Today we focus on a woman of the Bible. So, consider Sarai's nettles:

- Sarai lied about being Abram's sister instead of his wife (in obedience to Abram's advice).
- Sarai offered Abram her Egyptian slave, Hagar, to give him a child. (Genesis 16:2)
- Abraham accepted Sarai's offer. Jealousy and bitterness between the two women resulted in Sarai mistreating her slave and sending her away. (Gensis 16:6)
- Sarai laughed at the Lord when He told Abram she would have a baby "a year from now." After all, she was 90 years old and shriveled up. (Genesis 18:12)
- Sarai lied about laughing about it. (Genesis 18:15)
- Sarai went along with another lie — this time to Abimelech — about being Abram's sister, again in obedience to Abram's advice. (Genesis 20:1-2)

Did you notice in the verse from Isaiah, myrtle will come up instead of the nettles, and it will be a sign of God's power and love? God choked nettles out with the myrtle of His love. He even changed Sarai and Abram's names. Paul included both Abraham and Sarah in the rolls of the great Faith Hall of Fame.

---

[62] https://www.merriam-webster.com/dictionary/nettle (Accessed 9/27/2018)

> *It was by faith that even Sarah was able to have a child, though she was barren and was too old. She believed that God would keep His promise. And so a whole nation came from this one man (Abraham) who was as good as dead–a nation with so many people that, like the stars in the sky and the sand on the seashore, there is no way to count them.*
>
> ~Hebrews:11:11-12 (NLT)

Remember myrtle's symbolism of recovery and establishment of God's promises. God gave Abraham and Sarah's son, Isaac, the name Israel — the Jewish nation and family line from which Jesus came to earth. Through His death and resurrection, Jesus recovered for us all that we lose in our own poor choices, our sins, and our failures. He established the perfection of God's promises for our future eternity with Him.

> *You may be asking why I changed my plan. Do you think I make my plans carelessly? Do you think I am like people of the world who say "Yes" when they really mean "No"? As surely as God is faithful, my word to you does not waver between "Yes" and "No." For Jesus Christ, the Son of God, does not waver between "Yes" and "No." He is the One whom Silas, Timothy, and I preached to you, and as God's ultimate "Yes," He always does what He says. For all of God's promises have been fulfilled in Christ with a resounding "Yes!" And through Christ, our "Amen" (which means "Yes") ascends to God for His glory.*
>
> *It is God who enables us, along with you, to stand firm for Christ. He has commissioned us, and He has identified us as His own by placing the Holy Spirit in our hearts as the first installment that guarantees everything He has promised us.*
>
> ~2 Corinthians 1:17-22 (NLT)

God's promises are all "yes" in Jesus. They were to Sarah and Abraham. They are "yes" to us. And they are "yes" to our heirs, too. The Bible and history recorded for us how their story turned out.

Many times I have ask God about the purpose for the upheaval in my childhood. I have not received a definitive answer to that question, but I believe these words:

> *"Haven't I commanded you: be strong and courageous?*
> *Do not be afraid or discouraged, for the Lord your God*
> *is with you wherever you go."*
>
> ~Joshua 1:9

When I consider my children and their children and watch His plans for their futures unfold, I trust many purposes were and continue to be fulfilled with His "yes" just like He promised Joshua centuries ago.

As they did for Abraham and Sarah, Jesus and His/our Father provided many myrtles to replace the nettles of my life. In what areas of your life are you focused on the nettles? Pray and ask to see the myrtles instead.

Eucalyptus Essence Droplets

*Let everything that breathes sing praises to the Lord!
Praise the Lord!*
~Psalm 150:6 (NLT)

Fun Facts:

- There was a sprig of myrtle in Duchess Meghan's wedding bouquet.[63]

- Myrtle in the wedding bouquet appears to have begun as a royal tradition with Queen Victoria's daughter, Princess Victoria. Myrtle symbolizes hope and love, making it a fitting addition to any bride's bouquet, royal or not.[63]

- Fragrant flowers and leaves of common myrtle repel insects. They may help when used against mosquitoes and cockroaches instead of conventional insecticides in the homes.[64]

- Myrtle belongs to the same plant family as tea tree and eucalyptus, giving all three similar characteristics. In fact, myrtle's scent is reminiscent of eucalyptus oil.[65]

---

[63] https://www.townandcountrymag.com/society/tradition/a14401606/meghan-markle-wedding-flower-bouquet/ (Accessed 9/27/2018)
[64] http://www.softschools.com/facts/plants/common_myrtle_facts/1307/ (Accessed 9/27/2018)
[65] https://articles.mercola.com/herbal-oils/myrtle-oil.aspx (Accessed 9/27/2018)

Your Turn:

- Jellies and jams are favorites for canning, but I never thought of Myrtle Berry Jam before. Check it out.[66]

- Looking for a new confection recipe? How about Myrtle Berry and Rosehip Candies.[67]

- Grow Myrtle topiaries in your garden.[68]

- Refreshing on a hot summer day: Lemon Myrtle & Strawberry Iced Tea.[69]

- For a breathing refresher, diffuse myrtle or eucalyptus essential oils (or both together).

---

[66] https://domesticfelicityblog.wordpress.com/2016/12/17/myrtle-berry-jam/ (Accessed 9/27/2018)
[67] http://www.pennilessparenting.com/2011/02/myrtle-berry-and-rosehip-candies.html (Accessed 9/27/2018)
[68] http://toneontoneantiques.blogspot.com/2012/04/my-myrtle-topiaries.html (Accessed 9/27/2018)
[69] https://www.t2tea.com/en/au/recipes/recipe-lemon-myrtle-strawberry-iced-tea.html (Accessed 9/27/2018)

Chapter 7

Coriander
Trusting God's Sufficiency

Cinnamah-Brosia and Friends Share About

Coriander God Provided All She Needed

Diffusing Today: Coriander and Ginger
Aromatic Influence: The blend's calming affect may help to dispel fears and bring a sense of courage
Daily Delight: Zesty Lemon and Herb Guacamole
Musically: *I Am Trusting Thee Lord Jesus* (Traditional Hymn)
Verse of the Day:
> *And God is able to make every grace overflow to you,*
> *so that in every way, always having everything you need,*
> *you may excel in every good work.*
> ~2 Corinthians 9:8

Jane asked us to prepare our testimonies to encourage others. "As you pray about what you will bring to our group, be mindful how God teaches humility and trust in Him alone," Jane instructed.

Deborah remained very quiet in previous stories of life here at the Coffee Cottage, but she joined us every time. She surprised us tonight with an unexpected peek into her life.

"When my ex and I split up, I hired an attorney recommended to me. She was a tough one and kept pressing me to sue for alimony as well as an increase in the child support amount for 6-year-old Steven. Child support is based on current income, but she argued since he had multiple Masters degrees, it was possible for him to be earning more than he was. He should be held accountable. She thought he accepted a lower paying job to avoid more child support. I didn't believe that was true and told her why I felt that way. She kept asking. When we reached a final agreement, she even added a note stating that I was agreeing to the terms against her advice.

"Here's why I did what I did. I did not want alimony because I did not want to go the mailbox every month or check my bank account and be reminded that I could not financially take care of myself and of my child. If my state of residence at the time had not required child support to be paid, I may not have even pursued that. Of course, that would have been a mistake.

"The first couple years were financially tough. I needed the child support to pay rent and buy groceries. I never thought of my decision being out of pride, but I did learn a lesson in humbly accepting the blessing that child support provided.

"During the time of the divorce I did not push for more child support, because I did not believe my ex was taking lower paying jobs to avoid paying any additional support. I had no reason to believe he was hiding income or any of that. While I may have been legally entitled to sue for more, it just did not seem to me to be the right thing to do. I could have spent more time, and more money for attorney fees, and not been awarded an additional amount. It would have created a much more hostile atmosphere between my ex and myself.

"When it became obvious it would be helpful for Steven to have an adult male influence in his daily life, I was able to ask his dad if he would be able to take him. He agreed without hesitation. And, I began paying child support, even increasing the amount set by the court to help cover car insurance for a teenager. It seemed like the right thing to do since his dad had been faithful in making payments for nearly ten years.

"It will be 15 years this February since the divorce was final, and I have never ever regretted my decisions. I will also add that these decisions benefitted me as well. I was ready to put the marriage behind me and get on with life, so the sooner we reached an agreeable settlement, the sooner I was free. I guess it was a win-win of sorts.

"Through it all I have been very aware of God's hand in providing for us in good times and tough ones — and there were some of those! Any time someone suggested I had the right to ask for more, or I should go back to court, I still knew I made the right decision. God reminded me again and again that by remaining humble and trusting Him, Steven and I would be well taken care of. This made the journey much easier for all of us."

"Wow! Deborah, we all knew you were a single mom raising Steven. I remember you had some challenges with Steven in high school, and he went to live with his dad. We never heard you complain about your ex or bemoan your often, tight finances. The rest of your story is such a beautiful reminder that pride doesn't need to rule in the messy situations of life. Humbly working through them together for everyone's benefit better allows life to be a better place for all," Jane responded.

The Essence of Coriander in Scripture

What Is It?

Botanical Name: Coriandrum sativum;
native to southern Europe, northern Africa, southwestern Asia;
essential oil steam distilled from seeds

Being self-employed sounds really fabulous. Be your own boss. Set your own hours. Your time is flexible. In addition, you are often "all there is." Customers are your bosses. When there are none or few of them, your paycheck is slim. Your tax bite is higher. Worry, stress, and anxiety happily await an opportunity to invade your body, mind and spirit.

Dependence on your own abilities never cuts it. Great Big God owns it all. Trust in His sufficiency drops us humbly to our knees. Not in our faith or trust, but in His love for each of us, we find success and receive provision.

Two and one-half million Israelites left Egypt with many provisions and livestock. So relieved to be rid of them, the Egyptians probably threw it all after them — "Just take it all. . . please, and leave! Go! Get out of here!"

Stocked up for months when they left, the travelers knew they had it all covered. It took little time, however, to learn dependence on their own resources equaled failure. No place in that wilderness proved an appropriate plot to grow melons, cucumbers, leeks, garlic and onions like those they ate in Egypt. God moved them around often, too. They never remained in one place long enough to establish a garden anyway!

The Israelites whined and grumbled to their leader, Moses. And they blamed him. How like us. We know most often we have "more than enough," and still wallow in discontent. We fail to show humble gratitude for what we have.

> "Consider how the wildflowers grow: They don't labor or spin thread. Yet I tell you, not even Solomon in all his splendor was adorned like one of these! If that's how God clothes the grass, which is in the field today and is thrown into the furnace tomorrow, how much more will He do for you—you of little faith? Don't keep striving for what you should eat and what you should drink, and don't be anxious. For the Gentile world eagerly seeks all these things, and your Father knows that you need them.
>
> "But seek His kingdom, and these things will be provided for you."
>
> ~Luke 12:27-31

For the Israelites, provision came in the form of food falling from heaven. Did God provide the sustenance because the Israelites demonstrated great faith and humble trust? Not at all! He provided it in spite of their lack of trust and humility. They called the food manna:

> The community of Israel decided to name this mysterious substance "manna" (Which means, "What is it?"). It was white like a coriander seed, and it tasted sweet like honey wafers.
>
> ~Exodus 16:31(Voice)

The Bible verse indicates it tasted sweet like honey. It surprised me to learn cilantro and coriander are the same. Perhaps it tasted spicy-sweet?

It is suggested coriander helps one to relax during times of stress, irritability, and nervousness, and may provide a calming influence to those suffering from shock or fear.[70]

---

[70] Connie and Alan Higley, **Reference Guide for Essential Oils**, (Spanish Fork, Utah: Abundant Health, 1996-2012, Thirteenth Edition revised January 2012). Page 63

Go ahead. Try on the Israelite sandals. Walk a few miles in them. Are you experiencing fear, stress, irritability, and nervousness? Have you inquired what is for dinner tomorrow? In between the heavenly food drops, their shelves remained as empty as the cupboards in Old Mother Hubbard's shoe.

God's kids determined slavery appeared far more appealing than humble trust in God to see what He had in store. That seems difficult to imagine when, in hindsight, we realize He had just parted the Red Sea for them to walk through on dry land — not a bit of mud on their sandals. Previous to that, He sent many plagues to convince Pharaoh to let them go free. After they crossed the sea on dry land, God gulped up Pharaoh's troops in the same sea as its waves crashed over Israel's enemies.

When awesome times surround us we stand on top of the world because, "look what we did." When the bottom falls out or maybe we fall on leaner times we say, "God, what have You done to us? Why have you allowed this to happen to us?" What arrogance we show! How ungrateful we appear to be for everything He has done in our lives up to that moment. How unlovely we must appear to Him right then.

> "One of the mysteries of the gospel tradition is this strange attraction of Jesus for the unattractive, this strange desire for the undesirable, this strange love for the unlovely. The key to this mystery is, of course, Abba. Jesus does what He sees the Father doing; He loves those whom the Father loves."[71]
>
> ~Brennan Manning

---

[71] Brennan Manning, ***The Rafamuffin Gospel: Good News for the Bedraggled, Beat-Up and Burnt Out***, (Colorado Springs, Colorado: Multomah, 1990, 2000, 2005). Page 38

The Father loved His rebellious children, the Israelites; He loves every one of us, too. And too often we rebel, as well. We live far from super-spiritual lives just like those bratty children of Israel. Their provision could only be received in a humble posture. They knelt and gathered it from the ground — on a daily basis – and only enough for today!

When the Israelites arrogantly and greedily grabbed more than needed, God made the stuff rot. More than enough would not keep for tomorrow. They learned to live each day, aware that God cares about His ragamuffin kids. He did not let them down, and He will not let us down either, even when our trust lags.

> *"Jesus comes not for the super-spiritual but for the wobbly and the weak-kneed who know they don't have it all together, and who are not too proud to accept the handout of amazing grace."*[72]
>
> ~Brennan Manning

In the New Testament we meet Jesus as the Bread of Life.

> *"This is the bread which comes down out of heaven, so that one may eat of it and not die. "I am the living bread that came down out of heaven; if anyone eats of this bread, he will live forever; and the bread also which I will give for the life of the world is My flesh."*
>
> ~John 6:50-51

The children of Israel lived each day on the bread they called manna that fell from heaven. Jesus, the Living Bread, also came down from heaven. He sustains our lives forever!

---

[72] https://www.goodreads.com/quotes/7076043 (Accessed 9/28/2018)

A Woman of the Bible Humbly Trusts God's Sufficiency

Gathering So Much From So Little

Did I offer peace today? Did I bring a smile to someone's face?
Did I say words of healing?
Did I let go of my anger and resentment?
Did I forgive? Did I love?
These are the real questions.
I must trust that the little bit of love that I sow now
will bear many fruits, here in this world and the life to come.[73]
~Henri Nouwen

Elisha learned from his mentor, Elijah. He witnessed first hand the power of God at work in the lives of people through Elijah's ministry. God readied Elijah's heart to escort him to heaven. Before God whisked him away in a whirlwind with horses and chariots of fire, Elijah turned to Elisha and inquired how he could bless him before he was taken. Elisha asked wisely:

> When they had crossed, Elijah said to Elisha, "Tell me, what can I do for you before I am taken from you?" "Let me inherit a double portion of your spirit," Elisha replied.
>
> ~2 Kings 2:9

When a man dies his wife and children suffer. Without adequate financial preparations, difficulties multiply. The widow of one of Elisha's pupils found herself in that position. In defense of her husband, his calling as a prophet prevented him from financial gain. His embarrassed widow humbly trusted for help. Approaching

---

[73] https://www.brainyquote.com/quotes/henri_nouwen_588351 (Accessed 9/27/2018)

Elisha in a private conversation, she reminded him how much her husband "feared the Lord."

Women in general received little respect in the culture of the day, but I believe this woman saw a heart of compassion in Elisha's life. That observation bolstered her confidence to humbly ask for help. Without it, debtors stood ready to take her children as slaves since she possessed no other means to settle accounts.

Did Elisha boast a big trust fund or other financial resources? The Bible is silent on the point. The Bible clearly shows, though, he trusted the Spirit of God to provide. The widow trusted, too. Elisha asked simply how he could help and what did she have in her possession.

> *The wife of one of the prophets' disciples pleaded with Elisha.*
>
> **Woman:** *My husband who served you is now dead. He greatly feared the Eternal. You yourself know this to be true. The creditor is now trying to take away my only two children and make them into slaves.*
>
> **Elisha:** *What is it that you want me to do? Do you have anything of worth in your house?*
>
> **Woman:** *I don't really have much of anything. The only thing I have in my house that might be of any worth is a jar of oil.*
>
> **Elisha:** *Borrow as many large empty containers as you can. Ask neighbors for anything they can give to you. Be sure to collect a lot of them. Then enclose yourself in a room with only you and your sons. Pour oil into as many of the containers as you can. Set aside the full ones.*

The widow went away from Elisha and enclosed herself in a room with her sons. One at a time, her sons held a container before her, and she poured. Soon all of the containers were filled.

Woman: *Bring me another container.*

Son: *There aren't any left.*

It was then that the oil ran out. The widow then went back to Elisha, the man of God.

Elisha: *Now go sell the oil, and pay the creditor what you owe. Then your children won't be made into slaves, and you and your sons can live on the remaining money.*

~2 Kings 4:1-7 (Voice)

The difference between this struggling widow and the whiny Israelites emanated from trust. The widow pleaded out of the belief rooted in her heart. She trusted God's sufficiency. In spite of anxiety and concern, she turned to Elisha, the man of God, and asked for help rather than complain God abandoned her.

Like the manna God dropped from heaven out of love for His children, He also met the needs of the widow and her children. Both times He reminded us of His sufficiency to meet all our needs, too.

When have you believed your needs superseded God's ability to provide? What put you in that situation? Failure to trust? Poor planning? Over-extended credit cards? A circumstance totally outside your control? Trusting your own ability to provide over God's gracious hand? Go ahead. Insert a dozen more scenarios here from your own experiences.

God stretches each individual's faith to learn and trust, He always provides enough for today. Do we recognize "enough" as all we need? Often we look toward tomorrow with ungrateful hearts and over-taxed minds that question, "What if there isn't enough?" We hoard what we have, to live in a world of "wants" rather than true "needs." Build your trust in the truth of the Psalmist's words:

> *I have been young and now I am old, yet I have not seen the righteous abandoned or his children begging for bread.*
>
> ~Psalm 37:25 (NIV)

Manna from heaven or enough oil to pay the bills and live – we're never promised it will be easy, but we are promised God never forsakes His children. The manna (like coriander – and "what is it, anyway?") reminds us to leave our anxiety and stress at the door. Trust our all-sufficient God!

Coriander Essence Droplets

Jesus: I am the bread that gives life.
If you come to My table and eat, you will never go hungry.
Believe in Me, and you will never go thirsty.
~John 6:35 (Voice)

Fun Facts:

- Coriander is both an herb and a spice, because both its leaves and seeds are used for seasoning.[74]

- Size and shape of coriander leaves depend on their position on the stem. Fan-shaped, deeply lobed leaves can be seen at the base of the plant. Feathery leaves are typical for the flowering stalks.[75]

- Some people dislike coriander and describe its taste as soupy. Medical studies revealed that genetic constitution of an individual determines whether person will like or dislike coriander. In other words, genes predispose our fondness to coriander.[75]

- Leaves of coriander (also known as cilantro in North and South America) have fresh, grassy, lemony taste, while seed have sweet, nutty, warm and orange-like flavor.[75]

Your Turn:

- Do you enjoy curry dishes? Coriander seeds are one of the ingredients. Check out this link for a DIY curry powder recipe.[76]

---

[74] http://www.whfoods.com/genpage.php?tname=foodspice&dbid=70 (Accessed 9/27/2018)
[75] http://www.softschools.com/facts/plants/coriander_facts/1088/ (Accessed 9/27/2018)
[76] http://www.veggiebelly.com/2012/10/homemade-curry-powder-recipe.html (Accessed 9/27/2018)

- For those not into curry dishes, you might enjoy this DIY steak seasoning blend (coriander seeds included) instead. [77]

- Grow cilantro in your garden to harvest both the leaves and the coriander seeds (fruit) of the plant. Here's a guide for harvesting the seeds.[78]

[77] https://www.myrecipemagic.com/copycat-montreal-steak-seasoning-2502052078.html (Accessed 9/27/2018)
[78] http://bonzaiaphrodite.com/2009/09/spice-harvesting-project-saving-coriander-seeds/ (Accessed 9/27/2018)

Chapter 8

Orange Blossom
Keep Your Words Humble

Cinnamah-Brosia and Friends Share About
Orange Blossom
Kind Words Always Better

Diffusing today: Neroli (orange blossom)
Aromatic Influence: Helps encourage a place of confidence, courage, joy, and peace
Musically: **Words** (Hawk Nelson)
Daily Delight: Orange Pecan Bread
Verse of the Day:
> *Let your speech always be gracious, seasoned with salt,*
> *so that you may know how you ought to answer each person.*
> ~Colossians 4:6 (NLT)

Lily and Molly burst through the door throwing their arms around me in a giant squeeze of a hug! Their moms, Mandy and Amber, followed close behind. The girls chattered as the moms checked out the Orange Pecan Bread – today's daily delight. Conversations are commonly overheard at the Coffee Cottage. The girls' laughter drew attention as they talked about the events of their day.

"Can you believe Ms. Foster made them do that? It sure looked silly. Did you laugh?" Lily asked Molly.

"I held my breath so I wouldn't, but then I almost blew giant raspberries as I flip-flopped on the inside," Molly replied. "I had to hold my mouth and my sides at the same time!"

"I know. I turned backward for a few seconds while they balanced dictionaries on their heads and sang that song about how special they thought they were. I'm glad it didn't go on too long. I would have been in trouble, for sure. Of course, they deserved it."

Mandy and Amber caught the end of the conversation as they joined the girls at the table. "Why in the world would they have to do that, girls?" Amber asked.

"You know Ms. Foster just had a baby. We had a substitute teacher for a while. Some kids in our class were not very nice to the sub. Ms. Foster found out about the "very mean and bad boys and sassy girls," as the substitute called them. Ms. Foster had them stand in front of the class and balance the books on their heads and sing," Lily answered.

Mandy jumped in with the next question. "Were you girls two of the sassy ones?"

They shook their heads, but their expressions gave them away.

"Do you realize that when you are sassy you use your words in an unkind way? When you talk when it's not your turn your words do more to hurt people than help them. Sounds like the boys and girls in your class made it very difficult for the substitute to do her job. All of you learned less of what you needed to learn while Ms. Foster was gone. Now Ms. Foster must work harder to catch everyone back up."

The girls listened to Mandy's lecture with tears in their eyes. "It was funny to watch those other kids having to stand in front of the class like that. I guess they were embarrassed. I sure would have been," Lily answered.

Mandy added, "I'm glad she didn't ask us to do that. What's that big word that starts with an "h" when someone super embarrasses you about something you did wrong?"

"Humiliation," Amber responded. "But if you learn to be humble with your words — another "h" word – and talk when it's your turn and say nice words to other people, there's less chance for that to happen. When you are mean or sassy you tell someone you think you are better than they are. I know you know better."

Mandy suggested, "Would you girls be willing to talk to Ms. Foster tomorrow, and let her know that you were in on it too, and you are very sorry? You can impress her with your big new words, humility and humble, when you share the lesson you learned."

> *Pleasant words are a honeycomb: sweet to the taste and health to the body.*
>
> ~Proverbs 16:24

Note from Cinnamah-Brosia: Friends, Chapter 3 of the book of James in the Bible (New Testament) teaches much about our tongue and our words. If we could print a whole chapter of the Bible here we would, but copyright laws keep us from doing so. Instead, we urge you to read it from your Bible.

Orange Pecan Bread

I loved the flavor of this recipe from my childhood – the dryness of it, not quite so much. I searched several recipe sites and tweaked my family's recipe into something moister and tastefully pleasing.

Ingredients:

4 Cups All-Purpose Flour
1 ½ Cup Sugar
4 Teaspoons Baking Powder
½ Teaspoon Salt
4 Eggs
½ Cup Milk
½ Cup Butter (softened)
1 Cup Sour Cream
½ Cup Orange Juice
Grated Peel of 1 large Orange
¼ to ½ Teaspoon Orange Extract (according to your taste)
1 ½ Cups Chopped Pecans

Preheat oven to 350°. Grease 6 mini loaf pans.

- Beat eggs.
- Mix in the sugar.
- Blend in butter, milk, orange juice.
- Add sour cream and mix well.
- Combine dry ingredients (flour, baking powder, salt); add to the mixture 1 cup at a time until well blended.
- Stir in orange peel and chopped pecans until evenly distributed throughout the batter.
- Pour into prepared mini-loaf pans.
- Bake about 20-25 minutes until toothpick inserted in center comes out clean.

Allow loaves to cool at room temperature for 15 minutes before cutting. Serve with orange marmalade and/or butter. (Optional: Make a powder sugar and orange juice glaze and drizzle over tops of loaves.)

The Essence of Orange Blossom in the Bible
A Timely Word

Neroli: Citrus aurantium ssp. aurantium;
native to China, cultivated in the Middle East;
oil steam distilled from the blossoms

Junior High or Middle School years were rough. Words of others stabbed my heart like icicles many times. I mentioned in a previous chapter, I changed schools often due to many family moves. During grades six through eight I attended nine different schools. Being the new girl in class left me wide open to scrutiny. Everyone already had a best friend. Most often they excluded me from their circles.

One of the most humiliating experiences of my life arrived via a "Love Letter to a Mermaid." Dry scaly skin on my legs exacerbated by cold winter temps exposed me as a mermaid in the eye of some eighth grade boy. I remember little of his elaborate and sarcastic descriptions of his love for the "beautiful mermaid." What I do remember is how funny the teacher found the incident to be. She read the note aloud to the class, crossed out my name with several colors of markers, and posted the letter on the bulletin board for the whole world to read. How I managed to keep my eyes dry and sit through the nightmare eludes me.

My parents offered no suggestions for dealing with this. I preferred to never return to school again. That was not an option, of course. We lived with an aunt and uncle, cousins, and my grandmother at the time. An older cousin stopped by that day to visit Grandma.

She proposed a solution – at least to part of the problem. "Why don't you let her wear nylons?" If you're as old as I am, you remember girls wore only skirts and dresses to school – pants forbidden. I asked often for nylons. Mom and Dad declared them inappropriate for an eighth grade girl. After all, they were expensive and ripped easily.

This all occurred shortly before Christmas. My parents followed my cousin's suggestion. I found nylons in my Christmas stocking. I shared the story with my cousin a few months ago. Even though she retained no memory of the moment, her words sounded like sweet music to my ears at a time I desperately needed the encouragement.

> *A word fitly spoken is like apples of gold in pictures of silver.*
>
> ~Proverbs 25:11 (KJV)

> *"'Apples of gold' is a poetic name for the orange in more than one Eastern tongue. "Pictures of silver" may be a figure for the creamy-white blossoms of the orange-tree. No one who has seen orange-trees in full blossom and full bearing can have failed to notice how the beauty of the golden fruit is set off by its framework of white fragrant blossoms."[79]*
>
> ~Samuel Cox, D.D. from his work:
> "The Lessons of the Orange Tree"

You'll look long and hard to find much about oranges or orange blossoms in the Bible. The writer who penned the proverb quoted above, acquired first hand knowledge of their beauty and fragrance.

Kind words come from a humble heart, and endear the speaker to the hearer. Words laced with self-serving ego, anger, spite, pride, flippancy, meanness, and indifference build walls. Preconceived ideas about a person carry expectations of their behavior and speech. We may be ready to blow them off without giving pause to hear. Jesus certainly grabbed the attention and rattled the notions residents of His hometown held of Him. After all, He was "just" the carpenter's son.

> *Everybody noticed what he said and was amazed at the beautiful words that came from his lips, and they kept saying, "Isn't this Joseph's son?"*
>
> ~Luke 4:22 (PHILLIPS)

---

[79] https://biblehub.com/sermons/auth/cox/the_lessons_of_the_orange-tree.htm (Accessed 9/27/2018)

Their delicate nature and tiny size require the harvesters to harvest orange blossoms by hand. While enduring the several weeks of labor each year required for the task, the workers are greeted by the sweet aroma enveloping them in a mellow cuddle of joy, peace, confidence, and encouragement. Words perfectly timed embrace the hearer's spirit in much the same way. The word may even become the catalyst for a much-needed turning point in the hearer's life.

In the scene above Jesus taught in the temple. The Bible records many times and places His words came with perfect timing and changed lives. The woman about to be stoned for adultery serves as a perfect example. The Scribes and Pharisees about to perform the horrifying task question Jesus. They hoped to trip Him up with their legal opinions versus His. Jesus replied:

> *"Let him who is without sin among you be the first to throw a stone at her,"*
>
> John 8:7

The group slowly disbanded, and hopefully their attitudes adjusted after the encounter. Jesus next words spoken to the woman – like "apples of gold in a setting of silver" – infused energy to change her life:

> *Jesus stood up and said to her, "Woman, where are they? Has no one condemned you?"*
>
> *She said, "No one, Lord."*
>
> *And Jesus said, "Neither do I condemn you; go, and from now on sin no more."*
>
> ~John 8:10-11 (ESV)

The story is found in John 8:1-11. (I encourage you to read — or reread — her whole story.)

How do you use your words? Do they build up? Offer forgiveness? Encourage? Bless? Do you listen with your heart so your words offer a well-timed blessing?

Ironically this same tongue can be both an instrument of blessing to our Lord and Father and a weapon that hurls curses upon others who are created in God's own image.

~James 4:9 (VOICE)

Jesus speaks gracious words that empower us to be like Him, to make changes in our lives, and to encourage others. I challenge you to use your words thoughtfully and purposefully. That may not seem important to you, but the hearer's life may be changed forever. Jesus is our example. We follow His lead.

My cousin heard my predicament and my pain. She listened with her heart and offered words that bless my heart to this day. She forgot, but I never did.

A Woman of the Bible Humbly Listens and Speaks

Hearing Between the Lines

Speak in such way that others love to listen to you.
Listen in such a way that others love to speak to you.[80]
~Zig Ziglar

Upon the death of her husband and sons, Naomi spoke to her daughters-in-law. She encouraged them to stay in Moab, their home country, and remarry among their own people. One took her advice. The other, Ruth, found the friendship and counsel of her mother-in-law exceptional. Hebraic laws of the time required one of her husband's brothers to marry her to provide his brother an heir. Naomi's sons all died. There were no more. With little incentive other than the love between the two women, Ruth followed Naomi back to Bethlehem in Judah.

The custom sounds strange to our contemporary western way of thinking, but the kinsmen-redeemer remained a most important ordinance in Naomi's culture. Naomi envisioned little hope for the young woman.

Upon Ruth and Naomi's arrival in Judah, Ruth gleaned in the fields to gather grain to sustain both her and her mother-in-law.

> She picked up the grain and went into the town, where her mother-in-law saw what she had gleaned. Then she brought out what she had left over from her meal and gave it to her.
>
> Then her mother-in-law said to her, "Where did you gather barley today, and where did you work? May the Lord bless the man who noticed you."

---

[80] https://quotefancy.com/quote/943530/Zig-Ziglar-Speak-in-such-a-way-that-others-love-to-listen-to-you-Listen-in-such-a-way (Accessed 9/27/2018)

Ruth told her mother-in-law about the men she had worked with and said, "The name of the man I worked with today is Boaz."

Then Naomi said to her daughter-in-law, "May he be blessed by the Lord, who has not forsaken his kindness to the living or the dead." Naomi continued, "The man is a close relative. He is one of our family redeemers."

Ruth the Moabitess said, "He also told me, 'Stay with my young men until they have finished all of my harvest.'"

So Naomi said to her daughter-in-law Ruth, "My daughter, it is good for you to work with his female servants, so that nothing will happen to you in another field." Ruth stayed close to Boaz's female servants and gathered grain until the barley and the wheat harvests were finished. And she lived with her mother-in-law.
~Ruth 2:18-23

I hear love in Naomi's words. Boaz's role brought her pleasure. She cared about Ruth's safety and integrity, though. Naomi encouraged her to glean with the women rather than the men. The advice protected Ruth from potential harm. She listened and obeyed Naomi's words.

Naomi expressed timely words, fragrant with love and kindness, and exactly what Ruth needed to hear. The beautiful outcome: Ruth and Boaz married. Their son, Obed, became the father of Jesse, and Jesse the father of King David. Boaz's role as Ruth's kinsmen-redeemer honored Naomi as Obed's grandmother and the great-great grandmother of King David.

Wow! How's that for a legacy? Without Naomi's words of instruction to Ruth to work only with the women, imagine how the story may have ended quite differently.

Note: Ruth is featured in ***The Essence of Courage***, *Chapter 4: Saffron – Patience*

Orange Blossom Essence Droplets

A gentle tongue is a tree of life,
but a sinful tongue crushes the spirit.
~Proverbs 15:4 (NLT)

Fun Facts:

• Orange Blossom is the state flower of Florida (since 1909), and is the only state flower to be used in perfume.[81][82]

• Orange oil can be an effective grease cutter, and it has become popular in some commercial cleaners.[82]

• The Orange blossoms bloom in clusters of 1-6 in the spring and result in oranges the following autumn or winter. Last year's oranges often are still on the trees when the new Orange blossoms are blooming.[82]

• While highly aromatic, Orange blossoms taste unpleasantly bitter and may have a soapy flavor.[83]

• 1,000 pounds of orange blossoms are required to produce one pound of neroli essential oil.[84]

---

[81] https://mobile-cuisine.com/did-you-know/orange-blossom-fun-facts/ (Accessed 9/27/2018)
[82] https://www.theflowerexpert.com/content/aboutflowers/stateflowers/florida-state-flowers (Accessed 9/27/2018)
[83] http://www.specialtyproduce.com/produce/Orange_Blossoms_8808.php (Accessed 9/27/2018)
[84] https://www.air-aroma.com/blog/essential-orange-blossom (Accessed 9/27/2018)

Your Turn:

- In spite of its bitter soapy flavor, when used in certain ways orange blossom can be a tasty addition to foods. Here's a recipe for Orange Blossom Carrot Salad.[85]

- This recipe looks beautiful in the pictures at the link provided. Yours (and mine) may be less fancy, but still quite tasty: Orange Almond Cake with Orange Blossom Buttercream. When you make it, please post a photo on our Facebook page: http://facebook.com/lynnuwatson[86]

---

[85] https://www.simplyrecipes.com/recipes/orange_blossom_carrot_salad/ (Accessed 9/27/2018)
[86] https://adventuresincooking.com/orange-almond-cake-with-orange-blossom/ (Accessed 9/27/2018)

Chapter 9

Grapevine Pruning for Abundance

Cinnamah-Brosia and Friends Share About

Grapevine Lifted Up by the Vinedresser

Diffusing today: Fennel and Sandalwood
Aromatic Influence: Helping to provide a purified atmosphere of encouragement and harmony
Daily Delight: Grape Slushies
Musically: ***You Raise Me Up*** (Josh Groban)
Verse of the Day

But You, Lord, are a shield around me,
my glory, and the One who lifts up my head.
~Psalm 3:3

Our precious friend, Vickie, moved several states away a couple years ago — right before Miss Dot's Cafe reopened as the Coffee Cottage. Six months ago, she took a spill out the front door of her new home. The result: a badly broken ankle. A few weeks in the hospital, a couple surgeries, and lots of prayers later she was able to return home, but we sure didn't expect her to visit us here in Pearlville any time soon. Determined to visit her grandchildren, she made other plans. She showed up totally unannounced one Tuesday evening at the Coffee Cottage.

What a surprise. After hugs and laughter and lots of concern, we sat her down over in Wisdom Corner, where several friends gathered and chatted. We propped up her leg, and allowed her to get comfy. After a few minutes, Vickie interrupted the chitchat. She asked if she could pray for us, and then she had a testimony from this whole ordeal she hoped to share. Jane said, "Sure," gladly postponing any lesson she prepared for the evening.

Vickie prayed and began, "So when I first started this humiliating journey of helplessness, it was quite obvious to me that the message was the whole foot washing story. I was helpless to do anything, and people I loved had to wait on me hand and foot. And yes, that included very-very-very personal things. No choice. And then the challenge not to take it for granted to the point of demanding it at a certain time and certain way, etc. All of that is obvious. Yes? No?

"An event happened during the beginning of this journey that has had me mulling over what exactly God was teaching me. For many complicated reasons and major life stresses and lack of sleep and just an overload of being stretched beyond any sane personal limitations, my major caretaker just left. I didn't know what I was gonna do. But I knew however ugly it got I would survive. I still had one part time caretaker, but yes – part time. And I was helpless.

"Now what? Strangely, I was not panicked. I wasn't even angry. I prayed a lot for God to minister to this person. Eventually he came back but outwardly it seemed as if nothing had changed. My part-time help left, and this distant person was all the help I had. I had to completely depend on him for everything.

"He did everything and did it exceptionally well, and he never complained. Eventually he softened and we fell into a routine. Your caretaker has three jobs. Their regular job. Your regular job. And the care of you, which is about 80% of their time. It's insane and completely exhausting.

"You know what's hard? Watching them working so hard and you can do nothing to help except ask for them to do something else you can't do for yourself.

"So what is God telling me? A memory. My poor mother was in a position, which required much help. My brother sacrificed his entire life to take care of her. He needed my help part-time, and I balked. All I could see was my entire life being sucked down this empty hole, and I would never get to enjoy my kids and my grandkids and retirement etc. I was not very gracious. I ran away. And when I was there I was cold and distant. I finally came around, but it was too little too late.

"God said, 'I love you anyway. This person is willing to do for you what you were not willing to do for your own mother. You could not trust Me. He is trusting Me.'

"I am humbled. Humiliation and humbleness are different. Love humbles you. Indifference and anything less than love humiliates. God loves us beyond anything we could ever imagine, and He uses us to love others if we will let Him. If we will trust Him, laying down our own lives and picking up the life He has for us will be more fulfilling and joyful and better than anything we could ever imagine. And completely opposite from what the world defines as fulfilling.

"I finally am just now learning all this. Many have gone before me and learned it. They were an example and an inspiration to me. I hope and pray my life will also be an example and inspiration to someone else. It is a very hard lesson to learn. But our Heavenly Father is patient and lovingly teaches us."

For Vickie there was no party without confetti. Because she arrived unannounced, we had none to offer. Never doubt. Vickie brought her own and delightedly tossed it all around. We laughed and twirled in the swirls of color and sparkles and the encouragement she shared.

The Essence of Grapevine in Bible

Never Closer

Botanical name: Vitis vinifera;
native to the Mediterranean region

Grapes and grapevines show up in the Bible more than any other plant. This plant and its cultivation teach significant lessons. In the scenes leading up to Jesus' death and resurrection, we come upon two different mentions of the fruit.

In Chapter One we considered Jesus' humility when He washed the disciples feet and taught them to serve others. Immediately after their foot baths, Jesus and the disciples celebrated the Passover meal. As part of the celebration Jesus offered the fruit of the grapevine to them. He passed the third cup of wine of the Seder meal - The Cup of Redemption. He spoke these words:

> *In the same way, after supper He also took the cup and said, "This cup is the new covenant established by My blood. Do this, as often as you drink it, in remembrance of Me." For as often as you eat this bread and drink the cup, you proclaim the Lord's death until He comes.*
> ~1 Corinthians 11:25-26

Jesus served them the first Lord's Supper.

Jesus knew what He faced in the coming hours. He spoke many words of instruction and encouragement to His disciples during their dinner conversation. The disciples failed to recognize the messages He expressed.

Toward the end of the evening before all the crazy happenings of His arrest and conviction, Jesus shared these words with His disciples — more about grapes!

> *"I am the true vine, and My Father is the vineyard keeper. Every branch in Me that does not produce fruit He removes, and He prunes every branch that produces fruit so that it will produce more fruit. You are already clean because of the word I have spoken to you. Remain in Me, and I in you. Just as a branch is unable to produce fruit by itself unless it remains on the vine, so neither can you unless you remain in Me."*
>
> ~ John 15:1-4

Jesus demonstrated His own humility in washing their feet and in serving them the fruit of the vine (wine) representing His lifeblood poured out for them. His death demonstrated His most humble act of love for humanity. Amidst all of His last-minute and just-before-He-died-words, He says, "Remain in the vine, yield to the vinedresser, and produce fruit. And by the way, I am the Vine and My Father is the Vinedresser."

At this moment did the disciples roll their eyes? Did they think, "Oh yeah, He looks just like a grape vine – little squiggly tendrils and all!"

The disciples' joking aside, these combined moments of teaching provide powerful lessons in learning to live and love like Jesus did. At that moment I doubt the disciples had a clue.

A little research on growing grapevines turned up some interesting facts. This one really stood out to me.

The Greek word for "remove" in John 15:2 is the same Greek word used when the disciples "picked up" twelve baskets of food after feeding 5,000 people with five loaves and two fish. It means to gather or lift up.

> *Everyone ate and was filled. Then they picked up 12 baskets full of leftover pieces!*
>
> ~ Matthew 14:20

New grapevine growth trails down from the main vine. Left untended leads to a tangled mess. The vinedresser lifts the stems, tucks them in, and trains them. This discipline allows the sun to filter through to the grapes — the fruit. The more sunlight the grapes receive, the sweeter their taste. As the Father lifts those wild vines in our lives, He allows more of Jesus to be revealed in us. Our lives produce lovely fruit and lots and lots of it.

Pruning conjures up visions of severe cuts or wounds experienced by enduring all manner of devastating and trying times. And God may have reasons in the big scheme of things to press us harder sometimes, too. He must stand very close to us, nearly entwined with us to lift, tuck, and trim the unnecessary and unruly portions. Like the vinedresser tends the grapevines, God is the very closest to us when He does the lifting.

At one point in the course of that same after-dinner conversation, the disciples argued over who was greater among them. Jesus washed their feet, served them Lord's Supper representing His soon-to-be-shed body and blood, and reminded them no one was greater than another. They missed the point – totally.

We often miss the point as well, when the pruning seasons come. We see agony in the tough times and the difficulties. What He desires is closeness to us and us to Him – intimacy with the Father. In those moments, He says, "Humbly allow Me to move in your life in the way I know is best. I'll train you to reflect more and more Jesus' Light! Let it wash over you and spill out all over those watching you."

Remain in Him and be lifted up. Participate in His communion; serve one another with humility and joy.

A Woman of the Bible Humbly Growing Fruit

Mary Pruned and Lifted Up

*The vinedresser is never nearer the branches
then when he is pruning them.*[87]
~David Jeremiah

Have you ever considered how God pruned Mary, the mother of Jesus, just like He does us? Honorably engaged to marry Joseph, this precious young woman encountered an angel with a message, which derailed her plans. He brought unbelievable news that created totally unexpected challenges in Mary's life. That she believed the angel, and joyfully accepted the news, tells us she already lived a life that served God. Her life produced fruit. Did she know the difficulties she faced promised to produce the sweetest and most precious fruit all of mankind received — ever?

No one gets out of this world un-pruned — probably a gross understatement, right. Every person we meet in the Bible faced challenges like we do. (God — Father, Son, and Holy Spirit excepted.)

We understand pruning is a gracious act of God, because it trains us, moves our tangled and unruly motives and behaviors out of the way, and brings us closer to the sun/Son. We produce sweeter more abundant fruit. Choosing the woman to be representative in this chapter captured much more time and energy than I anticipated.

My choice surprised me. God led me back to discoveries in one of my own seasons of pruning. I shared the story in a blog post earlier this year. I refreshed it for the grapevine chapter.

On the first day of December last year my plans for the month crashed to a halt — literally. My car was totaled. Severe pain and trauma to my body necessitated a total reevaluation of personal, business, and holiday priorities. But not before I bemoaned all that was lost.

---

[87] https://www.azquotes.com/quote/864870 (Accessed 9/27/2018)

Car: *A TOTAL loss.*

Time: *All of it stolen away.*

My newest book, The Essence of Joy: *It gathered high praise and wonderful reviews on blogs, interviews, and more, but sales reports equaled flat line.*

My reflexology practice: *After a significant wane in clients during November, December promised to be even slower.*

Christmas decorations: *My extensive Christmas village was set up Thanksgiving weekend. Nothing else was ready.*

Christmas baking: *What a joke – nope none of that done either.*

Housekeeping: *Serious attention was needed in every area.*

And for 18 nights I slept sitting straight up on the sofa with a two-foot pile of pillows for support, a heat pad on my back and ice packs in front. While I could do little else, I spent time each morning writing out parts of the Christmas story from Scripture. I felt pretty sorry for myself, and lamented, "I need some angels to come fix my mess."

Then one morning spoke clearly to my heart: "But what about Mary and Joseph?"

They had plans, too. Wedding plans were underway. They anticipated a much easier trip to Jerusalem to celebrate the Feast of Tabernacles. Biblical scholars point toward this time as the most probable for the birth of Jesus. In The Tree of Life Version (a very literal translation of the Bible from the original languages) the "Word" did not come to "dwell'" among us – He "tabernacled".

> *And the Word became flesh and tabernacled among us. We looked upon His glory, the glory of the one and only from the Father, full of grace and truth.*
> ~John 1:14 (TLV)

Instead of a wedding and a fun-filled trip to the joyous festival, Mary and Joseph found themselves in an awkward, embarrassing, and scandalous situation: an out-of-wedlock and out-of-this-world pregnancy, detained for a mandatory census, and NO ROOM for them anywhere. And what OB/GYN or midwife would grant permission for a woman nine months pregnant to travel — on the back of a donkey no less?

Would you call that some serious pruning? But look what happens in the midst of their tough responsibilities and complications.

God sent a star and angels to interrupt lowly shepherds — GREAT JOY proclaimed at the birth of a Baby in a barn. The shepherds' hasty departure to visit the baby expressed evidence God provided and they witnessed the most magnificent Christmas lighting display ever and a birth announcement unrivaled by the most creative ones Pinterest™ has to offer.

God works behind the scenes lifting vines and cutting away the excess, keeping us close to Him. Always. And He always prepares a better outcome than we expect — sweeter more abundant fruit.

There were a few angels around my home, too. My husband put up the tree. (Not his favorite task.) Cookie angels arrived in various forms. I healed enough to do a few traditional Christmas activities. We replaced the car. We spent time with all our children and grandchildren, and we celebrated Christmas and our blessings with His joy in our hearts.

I contemplated the magnificent things God was preparing behind the scenes during this time of emptiness and helplessness – a time of serious pruning in my life. Many of my friends had their own serious challenges to face that same month, too.

While God prunes, He envisions the abundance. God is a God of renewal, regeneration, and resplendent harvest. I'm looking forward to surprises He has prepared for each and every one of us.

My circumstances required dependence on others to do what I could always do for myself. With humility I accepted their acts of kindness. My already honest compassion for those in a similar situation expanded even more. The weeks of healing brought me closer to God during the Christmas season when so many other things take over our time, lives, and priorities. I personally witnessed Jesus' spectacular birth announcement. My eyes opened in a new way to what the characters in the nativity story experienced the night of Jesus birth.

My abundant fruit comes nowhere close to Mary's experience. None of ours does. But life altering challenges and inconveniences motivate a reevaluation of our priorities and our plans. Seeing God's hand in allowing all that happens in our lives, prepares us to be used by Him to humbly minister to others.

> *We have become his poetry, a re-created people that will fulfill the destiny he has given each of us, for we are joined to Jesus, the Anointed One. Even before we were born, God planned in advance our destiny and the good works we would do to fulfill it!*
>
> ~ Ephesians 2:10 (TPT)

Grapevine Essence Droplets

But I tell you:
I will not drink of the fruit of the vine again until I am with you once more, drinking in the kingdom of My Father.
~Matthew 26:29 (Voice)

Fun Facts:

- Grapes are a kind of berry. They have a leathery covering and a fleshy inside, similar to blueberries.[88]

- Raisins are dried, sweet grapes. The drying happens naturally when the grapes are left in sunlight.[88]

- There are more than 8,000 grape varieties from about 60 species.[88]

- The oldest grapevine in America is a 400-year-old Scuppernong vine in North Carolina.[89]

- The grape appears in the top ten of the world's favorite fruits, along with tomatoes, mangos and bananas.[89]

- There are grapes that taste like cotton candy. I have eaten these, have you? They do taste like cotton candy.[90]

- The white wax you see on the grapes you buy from the grocery store is produced by the grapes, naturally. It is called epicuticular wax and it helps to reduce moisture loss.[90]

---

[88] https://www.webmd.com/diet/features/8-healthy-facts-about-grapes#1 (Accessed 9/27/2018)
[89] http://topfoodfacts.com/20-interesting-facts-about-grape/ Accessed 9/27/2018)
[90] https://www.kickassfacts.com/grape-facts/ (Accessed 9/27/2018)

Your Turn:

- Eat some grapes. They are on the list of top 10 favorite fruits.

- Roast grapes and serve on open face sandwiches. Here's a recipe for them: Roasted Grapes with Thyme & Fresh Ricotta on Grilled Bread.[91]

- Make your own grape jelly.[92]

- Create grapevine balls.[93]

- Build a grape arbor, and grow your own vines. As you learn about the process and techniques for pruning and growing grapes, apply those lessons to what we've learned about humility produced by being a part of the vine.[94][95]

- Watch a video about pruning grapes.[96]

---

[91] https://alexandracooks.com/2011/09/07/lunch-roasted-grapes-with-thyme-fresh-ricotta-grilled-bread/ (Accessed 9/27/2018)
[92] https://www.attainable-sustainable.net/easy-homemade-jelly-in-the-middle-of-winter/#wprm-recipe-container-6800 (Accessed 9/27/2018)
[93] http://www.the36thavenue.com/diy-grapevine-balls-tutorial/ (Accessed 9/27/2018)
[94] https://www.hunker.com/12000841/how-to-build-a-sturdy-grape-arbor (Accessed 9/27/2018)
[95] https://www.almanac.com/plant/grapes (Accessed 9/27/2018)
[96] https://youtu.be/0t6uXc2xEww (Accessed 9/27/2018)

Parting Thoughts...

Finally, all of you should be of one mind. Sympathize with each other. Love each other as brothers and sisters. Be tenderhearted, and keep a humble attitude. Don't repay evil for evil. Don't retaliate with insults when people insult you. Instead, pay them back with a blessing. That is what God has called you to do, and he will grant you his blessing.

~1 Peter 3:8-9

***If you loved this inspirational collection,
thank you for leaving a review.***

We love to hear from you, our readers:
- Sign up for our email list at http://LynnUWatson.com -- we will send you a FREE GIFT when you do.
- Visit our blog: http://LynnUWatson.com/blog We welcome your comments.
- Follow us on Facebook (leave comments and share, too, please) http://www.facebook.com/lynnuwatsonwriter
- And we are on Pinterest. https://www.pinterest.com/lynnuwatson
- Recipes featured at Cinnmah-Brosia's Coffee Cottage and gifts available in her gift shop are found on the website: http://LynnUWatson.com.
- In need of a website of your own. Thank you for considering http://www.watsondesign.us.
- Follow our cover artist, Allisha Mokry, on her blog: http://artfulexplorations.

Acknowledgements

Once again, I find myself indebted to many friends, family, and others who have given of themselves to make this third book in the Cinnamah-Brosia series a reality. And once again, I fear I'll miss someone important. My apologies. Every single person who contributed in any way is deeply appreciated.

Ditto my comments on this from previous books. My husband, Steve, has once again done a great job making this book look amazing. . . and created the beautiful book trailer, too! You continue to endure (and still love me) the adventures and misadventures of living with me. Thank you!

Allisha, Your talents amaze me! Who could resist the invitation from the friends on the cover to come join them for Cinnamah-Brosia's new inspirational collection? And the extra touch - the Cinnamah-Brosia paper dolls

Robin, you certainly had your own challenges during the writing of this volume of the collection. Still, I felt your prayers and knew you were rooting for me and for the book all the way through. I am majorly grateful for your insights before publication. Thank you!

Greta and Robin, thank you both so much for coming through beautifully in a moment of crisis. I love you both and your humble servant hearts!

Aryn, Charlene, Gladys, Jeri, Kandi, Michelle, Robin, Tanja, and Tiffany. A double-latte "thank you" for sharing your stories – they brought Cinnamah-Brosia and her friends to life, again. Without the stories there is no Coffee Cottage where friends gather to encourage one another.

My Family, you inspire me everyday. Once again I have used our stories and showed God's hand in our lives. I love you all so very much.

As always, "Ladies of Hope" and each lady in my Sunday School class, I love you all and am so grateful for your friendship, encouragement, and prayers. I am blessed God chose for us to do life together.

Amanda, April, Pat, Shirley, and Tanja – you read it first! Thank you for finding time in your busy schedules and for offering your kind words of praise.

    To God, our heavenly Father, be all the glory . . .

Resources

Richard Bauckham, **Gospel Women**, (Grand Rapids, Michigan: William B. Eerdmans Publishing Company, 2002

Connie and Alan Higley, **Reference Guide for Essential Oils**, (Spanish Fork, Utah: Abundant Health, 1996-2012, Thirteenth Edition revised January 2012).

Vincenzina Krymow, **Healing Plants of the Bible: History, Lore & Meditations**, (Cincinnati, Ohio: St. Anthony Messenger Press, 2002).

John Lawton, **Silk Scents & Spice**, (Paris, France: UNESCO Publishing, 2004).

Herbert Lockyer, **All the Women of the Bible**, (Grand Rapids, Michigan: Zondervan, 1967).

Brennan Manning, **The Rafamuffin Gospel**, (Sisters, Oregon: Multomah, 1990, 2000).

Lytton John Musselman, **Figs, Dates, Laurel, and Myrrh: Plants of the Bible and the Quran**, (Portland, Oregon: Timber Press, 2007.

Ann Spangler, and Jean E. Syswerda, **Women of the Bible**, (Grand Rapids, Michigan: Zondervan, 1999).

David Stewart, Ph.D., **Healing Oils of the Bible**, (Mable Hill, Missouri: Care Publications, 2003).

Allan A. Swenson, **Plants of the Bible and How to Grow Them**, (New York, New York: Kensington Publishing Corp., 1995).

Bruce Wilkinson, **Secrets of the Vine: Breaking Through to Abundance**, (New York, New York: Multnomah, 2001).

Other:

Many websites were used to gather the information in this inspirational collection. They are included as footnotes in each chapter. All links were active at the time of publication. If link is no longer available please use your search engine to find the info on another website.

Lynn uses the Young Living™ brand of essential oils. There are other quality brands of essential oils on the market. We recommend you research the options and choose high-quality oils within your budget.

Disclaimers

Cinnamah-Brosia is a fictional character. All similarities to real life people you know are totally intentional, but she is a little bit of all of us. Real women's stories were used and fictionalized (with permission) to flow with her character and the setting. We hope you found yourself and your friends right there on the coffee cottage pages. It's a great place to hang out.

For those reading this as an e-book, please know when converting to a digital file, spacing and format are very difficult to maintain in a book with much formatting like this one has. We've presented Bible quotes and other portions of the text for ease of reading in print format. Not all of that may have translated well to digital. Thank you for understanding and accepting our apologies.

None of the statements in this book have been evaluated by the FDA. The information contained in this book and in any references cited are for educational and inspirational purposes only. It is not provided to diagnose, prescribe, or treat or cure any health condition. The information should not be used as a substitute for medical counseling. Caution should be exercised when using essential oils. You are responsible for educating yourself and consulting with health care professionals in any and all matters regarding the use of essential oil or other plant-based products. The author accepts no responsibility for such use. Please consult with your health care professional for all your health care needs.

Some essential oils are unsafe or should be used with great caution for children and pregnant women. Consult your medical professional before use, and educate yourself about uses and cautions.

Young Living Essential Oils™ has not endorsed any part of this book. The author is not receiving any compensation associated with this book from Young Living Essential Oils™ or any other essential oil company. No essential oil company, including but not limited to Young Living Essential Oils™, is responsible for the information in this book.

About the Author:

Lynn Watson combines many years' experience in women's ministry, love of essential oils, and her passion for God's word to bring her readers freshly inspired encouragement for their walk with Jesus. Her devotional, *The Essence of Courage*, was recognized as a 'must read' by regional publishing industry leaders. Married since 1973, Lynn and Steve have filled their Bartlett, Tennessee home with handmade treasures and lots of love for family, especially their five beautiful (of course) grandchildren. Aromas of freshly baked bread often fill Lynn's kitchen. Jasmine, her tuxedo kitty, enjoys sleeping in Lynn's lap while she writes.

Dear Friends,

Thank you for hanging out with us at the Coffee Cottage. Welcome! Whether *The Essence of Humility* is your first visit, or if you have joined us for *The Essence of Courage* and *The Essence of Joy*, too, we pray your time here has been blessed.

We love watching our Coffee Cottage family grow. Please introduce yourself to us and share your own stories on our Facebook page. Just like at the Coffee Cottage, sharing our stories and yours encourages us all.

If you have never made a decision to follow Jesus, we encourage you to do so today. Pray a simple prayer. Humbly tell Jesus you know you are a sinner in need of His grace. Invite Him to come into your heart and make it is home. Attend a Bible believing church to plug in and grow. Find a mentor to come along side you in your faith journey. And please let us know of your decision, so we may pray for you.

Lynn's exhausted most of the flowers and botanicals of the Bible in the three volumes of this series. She prays the next major undertaking coming from her keyboard will be a novel, very loosely based on a real event from her family's history. The story takes place in the late 1800's. All Lynn has told me: The main character owns a cameo with secrets all its own.

Our door is always open and the coffee pot is always on – at least virtually. We love to hear from our readers, and welcome your comments on our Facebook page. You may email us through Lynn's website.

Hugs,

Cinnamah-Brosia

www.ingramcontent.com/pod-product-compliance
Lightning Source LLC
Chambersburg PA
CBHW052031070526
44584CB00016B/1997